STEP BY STEP TO

PERFECT GARDENING

MAX DAVIDSON

BOOK CLUB ASSOCIATES
London

Edited by **Robin Wood**
Designed by **Rob Burt**

All black-and-white illustrations by **Jan Churcher**
Colour illustrations pages 10/11 by **Juliet Stanwell Smith**

This edition published 1979 by
Book Club Associates
By arrangement with Marshall Cavendish Books Limited

© Marshall Cavendish Limited 1979

First printing 1979

Phototypeset by MS Filmsetting Limited
Frome, Somerset

Printed in Great Britain by Redwood Burn Limited
Trowbridge, Wiltshire

ISBN 0 85685 495 6

Introduction

Whether you have just taken on a new garden or you find yourself faced with a neglected one, it is a simple matter to start to put things right. Of course, there is no fast way to the perfect garden, but by doing the various tasks methodically, it is remarkable the transformation that can take place in a very short time.

Whether you want to plant a tree or some bulbs, the correct way of doing the job will often prove the simplest and the best means of ensuring that good results are obtained for your money and efforts. And on the subject of money, you can save yourself expense by referring to the chapter on propagating your own shrubs and plants. In fact, by following the right procedure, you can have a lovely lawn, beautiful roses and magnificent vegetables, all for a modest outlay of cash and effort. Here, too, are the answers to such puzzling questions as when and how should I prune, and what plants will be suitable for my garden? Whether you are a beginner or an expert, tackling the various problems step by step is the best solution I know to achieving the perfect garden.

Max Davidson

7	*Leslie Johns*
9	*Kim Sayer*
17	*A–Z Collection*
18/19	*Tania Midgley*
20	*Sutton Seeds*
27	*Miki Slingsby*
28	*Harry Smith Horticultural Photographic Collection*
29	*Michael Warren*
35	*Tania Midgley*
37	*Harry Smith Horticultural Photographic Collection*
41	*Harry Smith Horticultural Photographic Collection*
51	*M.C. Library*
52/53	*M. Newton*
55	*Ardea Photographic*
59	*Harry Smith Horticultural Photographic Collection*
61	*M.C. Library*
67	*Miki Slingsby*
68/69	*Harry Smith Horticultural Photographic Collection*
79	*Pat Brindley*
81	*Alan Duns*
82	*Bruce Coleman*
83	*Valerie Finnis*
87	*M.C. Library*
88	*M.C. Library*
95	*A–Z Collection*
96/97	*A–Z Collection*
98	*Roger Phillips*
103	*Bernard Alfieri*
110	*Alan Duns*
123	*Grant Heilman*
134	*Harry Smith Horticultural Photographic Collection*
139	*A–Z Collection*
141	*Harry Smith Horticultural Photographic Collection*
142	*Colin Watmough*
161	*Harry Smith Horticultural Photographic Collection*
163	*Shell*

Contents

Author's note: The naming of plants

In botanical classification the name of a plant consists of two parts. The scientific name of the maiden pink, for instance, is *Dianthus deltoides*.

The first part is the name of the genus (plural genera), that is the group to which the plant is related in sharing certain characteristics, particularly of its flowering parts. The genus *Dianthus*, for example, includes the plants we commonly know as pinks and carnations.

The second part is the specific name, that is, in the case of the genus *Dianthus* the name which distinguishes one species of pink from another (the maiden pink is *Dianthus deltoides*, the Cheddar pink is *Dianthus gratianopolitanus*, and so on).

In the text we follow the generally accepted convention of printing botanical names in italics, the genus capitalized but not the specific name. In the tables of suggested plants, however, we have used either the botanical or the common name, whichever is the most readily recognized.

The genus is not the largest category in the system of classification. A number of related genera make up a family. The genus *Dianthus*, for instance, belongs with a number of other genera (including *Silene*, campions, and *Cerastium*, chickweeds) to the family Caryophyllaceae. The genus is, however, the most convenient and generally accepted grouping of plants for a work of reference.

Within a species, distinct varieties may be known. Sometimes these occur naturally, in which case a varietal name is added, also in italics, to the specific name (e.g. *Dianthus carthusianorum multiflorus*). Where varieties have arisen in cultivation they are known as cultivars and are indicated in botanical classification by the addition of a cultivar name in single quotes and in roman type after the specific name (e.g. *Dianthus deltoides* 'Albus').

Besides natural varieties and cultivars many plants in cultivation are hybrids, that is crosses between species of the same genus, or more rarely, between species in related genera. Hybrids between species in the same genus are written with the name of the genus followed by a multiplication sign and the hybrid name (e.g. *Dianthus* × *allwoodii*).

A regional guide to seasons

In giving cultivation details, we have used such terms as 'early spring' and 'late winter'. By using the tables on this page you can find which months are equivalent to these terms in your region. Do remember to take into account any 'abnormal' weather such as a long winter, as well as the individual 'microclimate' of your garden.

UNITED KINGDOM

SEASON	South	North
Early spring	March	Late March/April
Mid spring	April	May
Late spring	May	June
Early summer	June	July
Mid summer	July	July
Late summer	August	August
Early autumn	September	September
Mid autumn	October	October
Late autumn	November	October
Early winter	December	November/December
Mid winter	January	January/February
Late winter	February	Early March

AUSTRALIA AND NEW ZEALAND

SEASON	Tasmania, mountains, Melbourne, Canberra, Armidale and South Island	Perth and Albany to Geraldton, N.S.W. Coast north to Kempsey, and North Island, New Zealand.	Coffs Harbour and north to Lismore, Brisbane, Bundaberg, Rockhampton & Mackay.	The Mallee, Wimmera, Riverina and the Darling Downs.
Early autumn	March	March	April	March
Mid autumn	April	April	May	April
Late autumn	Early May	May	Early June	May
Early winter	Late May	June	Late June	June
Mid winter	June/July	July	July	July
Late winter	August/Early September	August	August	August
Early spring	Late September	September	September	September
Mid spring	October	October	October	October
Late spring	November	November	October	November
Early summer	December	December	November	December
Mid summer	January	January	December/January	January
Late summer	February	February	February/March	February

First Steps

There is no easy way to the perfect garden. However, with a little thought and effort, it is quite remarkable what can be achieved. By planning your actions and taking the various tasks step by step you can have a beautiful garden and still have time to lie back on your chair outdoors on a warm summer's day. And think of the pleasure, as you sip a long cool drink, of seeing everything in marvellous order: the immaculate green grass, the flowers adding colour and fragrance, and the fruit and vegetables which help cut the food bills.

Nothing puts more people off gardening than the thought of its being hard work. Yet it need not be after the initial stages of preparation.

The first essential is to get the right tools for the job. It is amazing how a set of top-quality tools can make the various tasks seem easier, and if you take care of them by cleaning after use and wiping them down occasionally with an oily rag, there is no reason why they should not still be in perfect condition twenty years from now.

A spade is the basic implement which you will need for digging. However, there are numerous types of spades in various weights, sizes and finishes. You can get spades with stainless steel blades, for instance, which, although expensive, are invaluable in making light work of digging heavy clay soil. Some spades have handles made of wood; others of plastic. Get to grips with the spade before you buy: it must feel right if you are going to be happy using it.

Just as important is the right sort of fork. It will get a lot of use in the garden, breaking up soil which has been compacted by winter rain and doing an assortment of tasks from lifting potatoes to digging heavy soil or land which is full of stones. Look for a fork which has really strong tines made from the best steel.

A rake with a metal head is essential for levelling the soil and for breaking down the surface to a sufficiently fine texture so that seeds can be sown. A rake is also useful for preparing soil after winter digging and for making sure that there are no hollows when preparing a lawn for seeding. On an established lawn, use the rake to work in top dressings. And again on the lawn you will need one of those special spring-tine lawn rakes to do the job of scarifying, the removal of matted grass.

A hoe does a similar job to a fork in breaking up the surface of the soil, making it able to absorb air and moisture more easily. Your hoe will also get a fair amount of use in helping to keep down weeds. There are several types of hoe, but the best one for general use is the kind with a flat blade called a Dutch hoe. If possible, get one with a stainless steel blade. It is light and a joy to use and makes weeding less of a chore.

A trowel is the tool that you will need for planting all manner of things from bulbs to seedlings. Make sure you get one with a strong blade, as stony soil can soon distort a weak one. The trowel is often sold in a set with a matching hand fork, which is the best implement for weeding close to plants, where a Dutch hoe might easily cause damage.

If you have a hedge you will need a pair of

Right: A set of good-quality hand tools will make the various tasks to be done in the garden much easier to carry out.
Previous page: A busy but well-ordered town garden. The stone path leads the eye past the lawn, flower beds, ornamental trees and shrubs, and rockery to the fruit and vegetable garden at the rear.

shears, although many gardeners today prefer to use an electric hedge-cutter. You will also need long-handled shears for trimming lawn edges and keeping the grass neat around trees and shrubs. You will require hand shears, called secateurs, for cutting roses and most pruning jobs. Long-handled pruning shears, called loppers, are best for cutting away thicker branches and for getting at the centre of prickly shrubs such as roses. With really thick branches, of course, you will be better off with a saw.

A garden line is required to help you to make straight edges and neat rows when sowing seed. Choose one in bright orange polypropylene twine—it does not rot and can be seen easily.

A watering can with a fine rose will be needed for watering seedlings. You will also require a hose with a sprinkler attachment as nowhere can one rely on the natural rainfall to provide sufficient moisture in the summer months. Incidentally, you could consider getting a rainwater butt to collect the rainfall from your house roof.

A barrow may be necessary if your garden is large enough. In choosing a barrow, get one with a large, wide front wheel if you have no proper paths; otherwise you will make tracks on your lawn when transporting heavy loads. With a small garden, a plastic bucket is satisfactory for normal carrying.

A pressure sprayer to apply insecticides and fungicides will also be necessary to give your plants and shrubs protection from pests and diseases.

Finally, you will require a mower to cut the grass. Suggestions on that vital piece of equipment have been left until the chapter on lawns so that you can choose the most suitable type for your particular grass.

In addition to the basic tools, you can hire certain items such as power saws for removing old and unwanted trees, electric hedge-cutters and mechanical cultivators. You could make use of a cultivator even in a fairly small, new garden to rotovate the entire plot so that you can remove rubble and loosen the soil compacted during the building work.

But let us get back to basics. Whether you are starting from scratch or renovating an old garden, you need a plan of action. The first job is to get some graph paper and, using a scale of say 1 to 20, make a plan, showing the position of your house and those existing objects which you wish to retain, such as mature trees. Mark out, for instance, where you would like to have a paved area to sit or to sunbathe. It may not be possible to have this feature at the back door if your garden faces north. Decide too about a position for a greenhouse and possibly a sandpit for the children. This latter item can always be replaced with an area allotted to a garden frame at a later date. Make sure that the sunnier parts of the garden are given to fruit and vegetables. Sunshine for them is vital whereas there are many shrubs and plants which are perfectly happy in shade. Mark out too the position for a clothes line or rotary clothes drier if you want one. Then ask yourself some questions: How

(2) Avoiding a rectangular or square lawn in a narrow garden makes the garden seem wider. A compact fruit and vegetable plot is also an attractive feature.

(1) To plan your garden, put your ideas down on paper with a note of the approximate measurements of the various features you are thinking of including. Mark in the direction of the prevailing wind and observe which parts of the garden get most sunshine and at what time of day. This large, well-stocked garden (right) is sunniest along the righthand side.

much privacy do you want? Is there much point in putting up high fences when the neighbours can still see you from their upstairs windows? Are trees required to screen off an unpleasant distant view? Would a hedge be an advantage in providing shelter from the prevailing winds? How much of the garden do you want to devote to vegetables and how much should be left for flowers?

Once you have decided what you want, cheat a little. Take a look at what other gardeners have done in your neighbourhood and benefit from their ideas... and mistakes. Visit local garden centres in the summertime so that you get a better impression of what actual shrubs and plants look like while in bloom. And hopefully by reading *Step-by-Step to Perfect Gardening* you will find some suggestions which take your fancy.

Once you have a rough idea of what you want, put your ideas down on paper with a note of the measurements of the various features. By so doing,

you will save yourself a great deal of time and energy. For example, the area which will become a patio should not be dug over at all as such soil disturbance could cause subsidence later. Under normal conditions the soil for a lawn need only be turned over to a depth of 23 cm (9 in) instead of the 30 cm (12 in) or so required by vegetables, fruit and flowers.

In most gardens it is not necessary to concern yourself about drainage. That should have been attended to by the builders or the local authority. If it hasn't, get them back to fix it as it is nearly impossible to drain one garden satisfactorily in isolation. Similarly it is a waste of time to seek to have a lawn with a surface as smooth and as level as a billiard table's. It is far better to make use of the natural contours of the land and to achieve the occasional change in level, where necessary, with a retaining wall or a rockery which looks as if it could be part of the landscape, instead of simply a mound of earth and stones.

But before you get around to making any design changes or carrying out your master plan, let us take a look at your plot. All loose debris, bricks and large stones should be collected and put in a pile for later use as hardcore for a patio or under the base of a garden shed. If the plot is covered with coarse grass or a neglected lawn, this can be skimmed off in strips about 5 cm (2 in) thick and stacked carefully so that it will rot down and provide useful compost for feeding the soil later. The quickest way to get the turf to turn into compost is to stack the turf in alternate layers, grass side to grass side, with a sprinkling of sulphate of ammonia between the layers to assist the rotting process.

If the uncultivated land contains rough weed grasses, such as the one called couch, recognizable by its white, fleshy and invasive roots, the best remedy is to treat the area first with a proprietary selective weedkiller. Woody weeds, such as brambles, nettles, ivy and the sucker growth from

(3) For single digging, first dig out a strip of soil to one spit (one spade's depth). Move it to the other end of the plot being dug. It will be used later to fill in the final trench as you finish digging. Next dig across the piece of ground, throwing the soil into the trench in front. When digging, do not overload your spade and always bend your knees slightly. Try to develop a slow, rhythmic approach

which will enable you to get the work done without undue strain. (With a new garden you may have to go over the soil lightly with a fork before any proper digging can be attempted.) While carrying out single digging, soil improvement can be made by incorporating a layer of manure or garden compost in the foot of the trench before filling it with soil from the next trench.

old tree trunks, can be eradicated with a proprietary brushwood killer, which is watered over the area. The effect of both these weedkillers persists in the soil for about three months, but if applied in spring when the weeds are growing strongly, you could still have the plot prepared to sow grass seed in summer or early autumn, or to lay turf between late summer and late autumn.

Often the uncultivated land left by the builders is a mass of annual weeds together with more persistent perennials such as docks, dandelions and thistles. The most satisfactory solution to this problem may be to treat the entire area with a weedkiller containing paraquat and diquat: this kills the weeds and yet is rendered harmless on contact with the soil. The dead weed foliage can then be collected and burned. One application should wipe out most annual weeds, but others such as dandelions may need a second treatment after a couple of weeks. The great advantage of this weedkiller is that it clears the soil quickly and removes the necessity for much backbreaking work. Old and neglected gardens may also need this drastic treatment if the weeds have taken a firm hold.

However one vital warning: *all weedkillers are dangerous* to the user, children and animals. The instructions provided by the manufacturers must always be followed to the letter.

After the rubble and the weeds have been cleared you have to get down to the basic task of digging or forking over the soil. The latter course is often quite acceptable when preparing a lawn. So mark out the different areas with wooden pegs, according to your plan, to save yourself unnecessary effort.

Should the soil be stony, or if there is an impervious layer of compacted soil and stones—known to gardeners as hard pan—just below the surface, normal digging may be impossible and special treatment may be required. The easiest solution is to hire a mechanical cultivator with toughened digging blades to deal with such con-

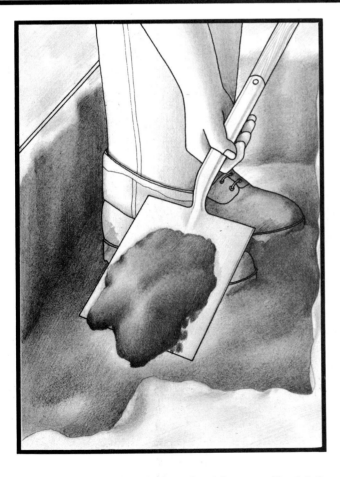

(4) Double digging is invaluable on soil which is poorly drained and also on soil which is to be used to grow vegetables. Take out a trench as for single digging.

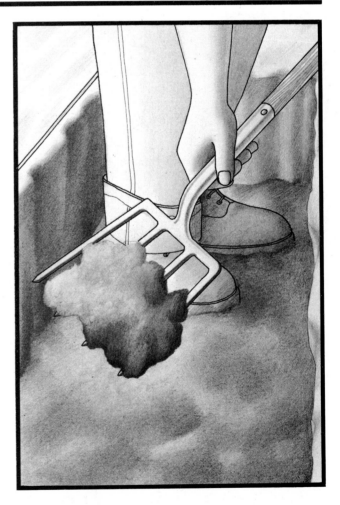

(5) Then fork over the soil at the base of the trench before adding manure or compost.

13

ditions. The alternative is to fork over the soil to a depth of about two spits and to leave the soil rough so that it is exposed to the effects of rain, wind and frost. [A spit is a gardener's term denoting one spade's or fork's depth of soil—a conventional spit is 25 to 30 cm (10 to 12 in).]

Heavy clay soils are best dug between late spring and early winter. Never attempt to dig them when they are wet and sticky. You will only make matters worse as well as giving yourself backache. Light sandy, loamy or peaty soils can be dug at any time when the weather is favourable for gardening.

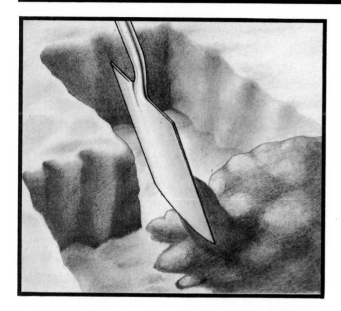

(6) Next dig across the plot, throwing the soil into the trench in front. Leave the lumps of soil large so that they will present a greater surface area to the action of wind, rain and frost.

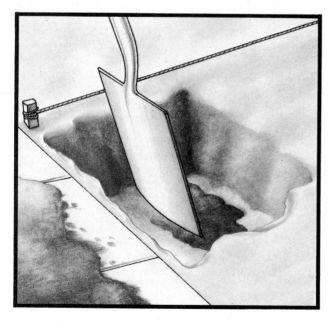

(7) Continue in this way until you reach the end of the plot where the soil taken from the first trench should be used to fill the final trench.

14

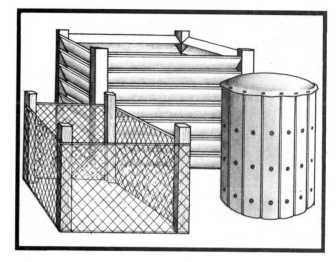

(8) Compost can be made only in a properly constructed heap. For the majority of gardens it is best to buy a couple of plastic or wire compost bins. Alternatively you can make them from plastic fencing netting and sturdy posts. The minimum satisfactory size is a cubic metre (about a cubic yard). All organic matter, weeds, leaves, grass cuttings and household vegetable waste can go on the heap.

(9) The way to produce good compost is to build up the heap in layers of well-mixed materials like a sponge cake. Avoid excessive amounts of wet grass clippings at any one

The texture of any soil, be it clay or sand, can be partially determined or improved by the addition of organic matter, which breaks down in the soil to form humus. Humus helps the soil to absorb air and moisture. It also nourishes the bacteria which convert fertilizers into a form readily assimilated by plants' root systems.

That life-giving organic matter can be supplied in several ways. In country districts you can use farmyard manure, which is not always easy to obtain. It is far better to use your own garden compost made in properly constructed heaps. For

point in the heap as this will upset the even decomposition of the heap. Similarly if you are likely to have a large amount of autumn leaves, consider having a separate heap purely for leaves which will eventually turn into valuable leaf mould for mulching shrub beds. Too many leaves in a normal heap upset the rotting process. Each 23 cm (9 in) layer of the heap should be sprinkled with a compost activator, but do not add any garden soil. Water may be necessary to wet certain materials if the weather is dry, but apart from that resist the temptation to tamper with the heap until that pleasant earthy smell tells you that the compost is ready for use. The actual time taken for the compost to mature depends on the time of year the heap was started and also on the surrounding temperature. Thus, a heap started in spring should be ready in autumn; while one begun in autumn may take the best part of a year to reach maturity.

(10) A soil-test kit will tell you whether your soil is alkaline or acid. By adding various chemicals to a sample of soil in a prescribed order and comparing your results with the colour charts provided with the kit, you can also discover if your soil is deficient in nitrogen, phosphorus or potash. The best time to add lime to the soil is in autumn or winter. Fertilizers should be added in spring and summer in the amounts determined by your soil test.

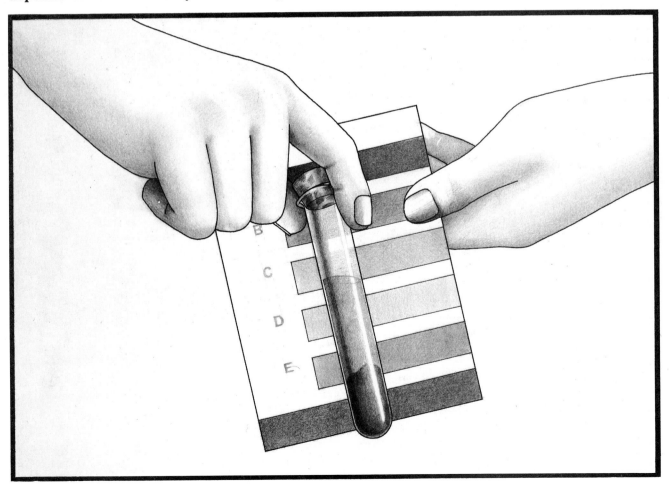

most gardens, at least two heaps are required because of the irregular supply of material and the effect of the climate on the rotting-down process. Most new gardens are unlikely to have sufficient organic material to make all the compost wanted. So you will have to make use of substitutes such as peat, shredded bark and spent hops to improve the condition of the soil.

As well as improving the physical structure of the soil, garden compost also provides some plant nutrients and is thus indispensable to the average gardener as a readily available source of mulch. Mulch is a cover spread over the surface of the soil, either to inhibit weed growth, to help retain moisture, or to help improve the level of nutrients in the soil. Besides garden compost, materials for mulching include farm manure, peat, straw and sheets of black polythene, depending on what is available and the plant to be mulched. A well-mulched garden needs less time and work to keep it weed-free and watered.

Peat, shredded bark and spent hops, however, provide little plant food at all and may actually use up some of the existing nitrogen in the soil as they decompose to form humus. Consequently many gardeners make good the soil's need for certain plant foods by adding chemical fertilizers.

There are three main chemicals required by plants: nitrogen, phosphorus and potassium.

Nitrogen produces growth. If a plant is getting too little nitrogen, it will be stunted and the leaves will be small and yellowed. If too much is made available, the growth will be soft, lush and leafy. Nitrogen, in a form acceptable to the plant, is taken up by the roots as the result of bacterial action. Most nitrogen fertilizers are very soluble and can be washed away rapidly by heavy rain. Consequently it pays to add them little and often. Chemical sources of nitrogen are sulphate of ammonia, nitrochalk and nitrate of soda, all of which are quick acting. Away from the vegetable plot it is much better to use an organic source of nitrogen such as hoof and horn meal, dried blood, or meal made from fish scraps. Although these are expensive, they are longer lasting.

Phosphorus, in the form of soluble phosphates, is necessary for good root formation. If the soil is short of phosphate, the leaves of plants will be dull and growth will be slow. Superphosphate of lime is the usual chemical source of phosphate. Steamed or sterilized bonemeal, as well as being an organic phosphate source, also supplies nitrogen.

Potassium in the form of potash assists the ripening of fruit and vegetables and improves the intensity of flower colour. It also increases a plant's resistance to pests and diseases and hardens the tissues, enabling it to survive unscathed during prolonged cold and wet weather. A potash deficiency is shown by a scorched appearance at the leaf edges. Light soils are most likely to be short of potash and the best source is sulphate of potash.

There are a number of fertilizers which are sold in compound form to suit various groups of plants. A general fertilizer, for example, is fine for vegetables, fruit and flowers. However, you will get better results from your roses if you use a specific rose fertilizer containing magnesium and different proportions of the same ingredients as the general fertilizer. Similarly, lawn fertilizers are often composed of slow-release chemicals which feed the grass over several months and avoid scorching the lawn. All fertilizers, however, are expensive and it is wise to buy a simple soil-test kit to check what exactly your soil requires before you actually start to add anything.

A soil-test kit will also let you know if your soil is alkaline and has plenty of calcium, which is normally added when necessary in the form of lime. Alternatively a test may reveal that little if any calcium is present and that the soil is acid. This information is vital in determining the type of vegetables, fruit and flowers which you can grow in your garden. Cabbages, plums and bulbous irises are good examples of plants which do best in soil containing lime or chalk, whereas potatoes, strawberries and lupins need an acid soil. Fortunately most soils are fairly neutral and provide the most suitable conditions for the vast majority of plants. The soil in natural limestone or chalk districts is likely to be alkaline. Acid soils are normally sandy or peaty. However, some clay soils are also acid. Hence the necessity to use a soil-test kit. With regard to the lime test your result will be expressed in terms of the pH factor which is a chemist's way of indicating the degree of acidity or alkalinity of the soil. A pH of 7 is regarded as neutral. Normally the scale runs, so far as gardens are concerned, from pH 4.5, which is very acid, to pH 7.5, which is alkaline. Ideally you should aim to keep your soil at pH 6.5 which suits most plants. It takes 2 kg of lime to 10 sq m (5 lb to 11 sq yd) to change the pH value from 6.75 to 7.5, for example. The process can be reversed by applying sulphate of ammonia at the rate of 750 gm to 10 sq m (1½ lb to 11 sq yd). The same acidifying effect can be obtained by adding moss peat at the rate of 15 kg to 10 sq m (35 lb to 11 sq yd).

16

The Lawn

Healthy, green grass gives a well-cared-for look to any garden. A beautiful lawn enhances your home as well as being the perfect foil for all the other plants, shrubs and trees. Producing the perfect lawn is not cheap or easy. Yet, thanks to the many modern garden aids, you will be amazed what can be achieved with a little patience and forethought.

The real secret of a successful lawn is to have properly prepared soil from the start. It is often forgotten that grass is a plant which needs the same feeding and care as any other if it is to grow well. In fact, if you consider what is demanded of grass, it should by rights merit some extra special attention. Regular mowing and the elimination of pests and weeds also assist in attaining the desired result.

The first question you have to ask yourself is whether to make a lawn from turf or seed. Turf certainly provides the quickest method of obtaining a usable lawn, but unless the turf can be purchased specially grown from seed, it could provide you with a considerable number of headaches. Avoid in particular offers of cheap meadow turf, containing undesirable grasses and weeds.

Seed offers the cheapest and most satisfactory way to make a lawn. For the great advantage of seed is that it enables you to suit the actual grasses to your soil and purpose. You could, for example, use a seed mixture containing fine-bladed species of grass for a front lawn which would get very little wear. Such a mixture of grasses would produce an ornamental lawn with the appearance of a bowling green. There are snags of course with this type of grass mixture. Firstly the lawn must be kept trimmed at least once a week. Secondly the lawn will require a regular programme of feeding and watering during dry spells.

The most popular lawn for the average garden is produced by sowing a mixture of fine and hard-wearing, dwarf broad-leaved grasses. This kind of lawn looks good and resists wear, a factor lacking in the ornamental lawn.

Next there is the kind of grass mixture which contains a high proportion of broad-leaved grasses, including some perennial rye-grass. This type of lawn may never be beautiful, but it will be sufficiently hard-wearing to resist the activities of boisterous dogs and children playing. Such grass seed mixture also grows quickly and it is the best choice for poor, clayey soils if you do not wish to spend the money to make the necessary soil improvements to suit a finer seed mixture.

It is also possible to obtain grass seed mixtures suitable for densely shaded areas, which will provide a beautiful green carpet of grass if not mown too closely.

Whatever method you choose to make a lawn, it will succeed only if you prepare the soil thoroughly. After the site has been cleared of all weeds and rubble, dig a couple of holes about two spits deep at opposite ends of the intended lawn when rain is

expected. The idea is to test whether or not water drains away freely. If it does not, those holes will still contain water several hours after all rainfall has ceased. By making those holes you will also get some necessary information on the soil structure and possibly the subsoil. If conditions are normal, it will be sufficient to dig, rotovate or fork over the soil to a depth of 23 cm (9 in). If, however, you discover

18

drainage problems, or a hard pan of compacted soil, below the surface, double digging as described in Chapter One will be required.

Should your soil be light, or clayey yet well-drained, peat should be forked in at the rate of 3 kg per sq m (5½ lb to a sq yd) to help it to retain moisture. Clay soil has the disadvantages of being wet in winter and also drying out excessively in hot

Previous page and above: Whatever the size and shape of your garden, a lawn is restful to the eye and provides useful open space.

summers. If your soil is heavy, putty-like clay, then weathered cinders, coarse river sand or fine gravel should be spread over the entire lawn area to a depth of about 5 cm (2 in) and then forked in to

19

Above: Regular mowing and attention to pests and weeds help to achieve a lovely lawn.

loosen the texture and to assist drainage. With such conditions, you could also consider going over the area a second time, if it is not too large, forking some peat into the top few centimetres of soil. It is a great deal of effort, but the results in a matter of months will make it seem all worth while.

The lawn surface should be levelled, when the soil is sufficiently dry to walk on without its sticking to your shoes, by raking and treading with your heels. Do not under any circumstances use a roller or you will destroy all the hard work you put in by forking or digging over the soil. Continue this raking and treading over a couple of weeks until the soil has a fine crumbly appearance and all hollows have been eliminated. Do not concern yourself too much about stones. Remove only those larger than a golf ball. It is a mistake to sieve the soil finely as after a heavy downpour you will find yourself faced by a sea of mud. Similarly do not worry if there is a sudden growth of annual weeds on the lawn area prior to sowing. The simple solution is to treat them with a herbicide containing paraquat and diquat which is rendered harmless on contact with the soil.

Grass seed can be sown any time between mid-

spring and early autumn. Late summer sowings have the advantage that the soil is warm and the seed germinates rapidly. Fewer weeds grow during the autumn and winter and there is usually enough rain. Also if you have young children, they are less likely to want to play outdoors in the cold and wet of autumn and winter. So by the following spring, a lawn sown in late summer or early autumn is thick and ready to walk on. Mid-spring, however, may be the best time for sowing in cool, higher latitude districts where the lack of daylight in autumn and winter leads to poor grass growth.

A day or two before sowing or turfing scatter a general fertilizer over the site at the rate of 56 gm per sq m (2 oz per sq yd) and rake lightly in. For accurate sowing mark out the plot with string into metre (yard) wide strips. Then sow the seed at the rate of 42 to 56 gm per sq m ($1\frac{1}{2}$ to 2 oz to a sq yd). To save time and seed, get a small jar and, using kitchen scales, mark on the side of the jar the appropriate measure of seed.

After sowing, the soil can be gently raked to cover the seed lightly but on no account should the seed be deeply buried; otherwise it will fail to germinate.

Grass seed is usually sold treated with a chemical to make it unpalatable to birds, but harmless to children and pets. On hot, dry days birds may attempt to take dust baths in your newly sown lawn.

The answer is either to keep the soil damp by sprinkling it with water, or, if it is a small lawn, to use black cotton thread wound around small stakes and covering the entire area. In any event lawns sown from late spring to late summer may need to be watered regularly to ensure good germination, which under normal conditions takes one to two weeks, as a sudden drought can kill the seedlings before the roots are fully developed.

Achieving an 'instant lawn' by laying turf is very expensive, but may recommend itself for the small garden. Turf can in theory be laid at any time but newly laid turf will need to be watered frequently if the weather is dry. For this reason, the best results in practice are achieved in early spring and autumn.

Once your new grass—whether grown from seed or turf—has reached a height of 5 cm (2 in) it can be cut lightly with a mower to reduce it to 2.5 cm (1 in). This first cut should be made when the grass is perfectly dry, and the clippings should be collected

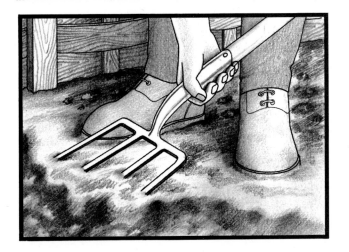

(1) Whether sowing seed or laying turf, under normal soil conditions all that should be necessary is simply to fork the soil over to a depth of 23 cm (9 in), thus saving yourself a considerable amount of work. Depending on the soil, you may also have to add peat and/or weathered cinders, coarse river sand, or gravel, to improve the moisture-retaining ability or drainage of the soil. Sandy and chalky soils are most likely to be in need of the addition of liberal quantities of peat. Clay soil is almost certainly likely to need some improvement to its drainage.

carefully marked out with wooden pegs or with pegs and string so that you can continue if necessary with the cultivation of other parts of the garden without disturbing your lawn construction. If you want to be sure of a level surface, mark a line 10 cm (4 in) from the top of each peg and hammer the pegs into the ground to indicate the desired soil level. If necessary, lay a straight-edged board across two pegs and place a spirit level on the board to make sure that the pegs are at the same height. Then add or remove soil from between the pegs until the soil surface is level with the line marked on each peg.

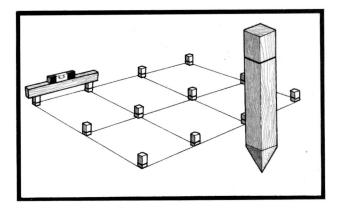

(2) The area of the proposed lawn should be

(3) When the soil is sufficiently dry to walk on without it sticking to your shoes, the surface should be levelled by raking and

in the mower's grass box, or gently raked off the new lawn with a spring-tined rake.

There is a wide selection of mowers available with either cylinder or rotary blades. Most mowers today are powered (either by petrol or electricity) and there are powered machines suitable even for very small lawns, so that grass cutting is no more arduous than vacuum-cleaning a carpet. Your best plan is to choose a mower which picks up the clippings, as clippings left on the lawn are bad for the health of the grass as well as being a nuisance when they are blown on to paths and flower beds and carried by feet into the home. Those much-admired stripes on lawns are produced by mowers with rear rollers, which also allow you to cut right up to lawn edges.

Rotary mowers give best results with less-than-perfect grass. They are also ideal in areas of high rainfall where the grass often has to be cut while it is wet. Some are useful too on lawns on steep

---

treading with your heels. Continue with this raking and treading until the soil has a fine crumbly appearance and all the bumps and hollows have been removed.

(4) For sowing, the lawn area should be marked out with string into 1 metre (1 yard) wide strips to enable you to sow the correct amount of seed accurately.

(5) Sow the seed at the rate of 42 to 56 gm per

sq m (1½ to 2 oz per sq yd), north to south and east to west, in each marked-out area in order to obtain the most even distribution. Then, after sowing, rake the soil very lightly, taking care to make sure that the seed is not buried too deeply.

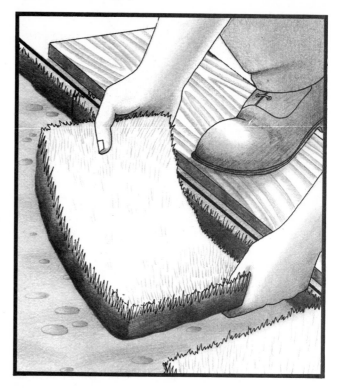

(6) Turf is usually supplied cut in 30 cm by 90 cm (1 ft by 3 ft) strips. After taking delivery, stack the turf ready for use carefully so that the strips do not get broken. When turfing, start at one end of the proposed lawn and lay in straight rows, using a garden line to guide you. Stagger the turfs in alternate rows like bricks in a wall. However, avoid using small sections at the lawn edges where they are easily disturbed. Stand on a plank while you work to prevent the soil from becoming too compacted.

slopes and for cutting grass under and around shrubs and trees. However, for the finest possible finish on ornamental lawns, the 'old-fashioned' cylinder mower is still the best choice.

Regular mowing encourages the finer grasses and reduces the number of coarse grasses in the turf. Never allow the grass to get so long before cutting that you are left with an unpleasant yellow and white patchwork appearance once the lawn is mown. Mow at least once a week between mid-spring and mid-autumn and occasionally in mild winters if the grass shows signs of growth. Always vary the direction of mowing over the course of the year so that you catch the blades of grass from differing angles and get the smoothest finish. Most lawns should never be cut any shorter than 2 cm ($\frac{3}{4}$ in), as a shaved finish, unless expertly done and the grass watered and fed regularly, will inevitably lead to an unattractive, brown patched lawn for much of the summer.

(7) Check that each turf lies against its neighbour and make the necessary adjustment by adding or removing soil from under the turf. It is useful to have a garden barrow close by with a supply of soil for this purpose. As you proceed, beat down the turfs lightly with a back of a spade to make sure of firm contact with the soil.

(8) Once all the turfs are laid, fill in all the cracks between them with a mixture of moist peat and good soil to encourage them to knit together. The peat-and-soil mixture can either be brushed into the cracks or worked in with the back of an ordinary rake.

(9) Uneven edges can ruin the overall effect of a lawn. Use a garden line to mark out a straight edge and place a board close to the garden line. Then make neat cuts with your spade or half-moon lawn-edging tool. If you wish to cut curves, secure the garden line in the desired shape with small wooden pegs. Every time you cut the lawn, also cut the ragged grass at the edges with long-handled shears.

Mowing is the main chore in lawn care, but the overall effect can be ruined if the edges are untidy. You can do away with the need to trim lawn edges by setting small paving slabs or bricks slightly lower than the turf during the construction of the lawn. If you do have edges to trim, keep them neat by placing a board at the edge of the lawn and cut the turf cleanly once a year with either your spade or a lawn-edging tool. Then every time you mow the grass, clip the edges with edging shears.

If you continue to cut the lawn without feeding it, it soon becomes pale, weedy and infested with moss. Regular feeding is essential. The best plan is to use a proprietary lawn fertilizer in mid-spring and early autumn. Fertilizer can be applied by hand, but a more even distribution can be obtained with a special lawn spreader. Do make soil tests from time to time to check if certain plant foods are lacking, in which case you may have to correct the condition with an application of a specific

(11) Like all other plants, grass will not flourish unless air and water can reach its roots. Even a lawn which is cut regularly with a mower with a grass box tends to form a mat of dead foliage on the soil surface which resists the passage of air and water to the roots. This matted grass, or 'thatch', should be removed in spring and autumn with a spring-tined rake. There is no need to scrub vigorously at the lawn. A light sweeping movement is quite sufficient.

(10) The simplest and the best way to make certain that your lawn is evenly fed is to use a fertilizer spreader. Work in a regular pattern of strips, checking that you have neither an excessive overlap of double-dosed areas nor missed sections. If it is impossible to start using the spreader up and down the lawn because of flower beds or walls, mark off a couple of spreader widths. Then treat the rest of the lawn before returning to the marked off section. This will avoid the possibility of double dosage which results in scorched grass and uneven growth.

(12) If a lawn develops mossy patches, the cause is usually either lack of feeding or poor

straight fertilizer such as sulphate of ammonia to rectify a nitrogen deficiency. Sulphate of ammonia is best dissolved in water and applied by a watering can during spring and early summer.

Nitrogenous fertilizers such as sulphate of ammonia, however, must not be used after late summer. Autumn feeding should be carried out only if the lawn has become compacted or has suffered from drought. For autumn feeding, spread a proprietary fertilizer rich in phosphates (but low in nitrogen) over the lawn to encourage a healthy root system.

A plentiful supply of water is vital to keep your grass in top condition. There is a variety of sprinklers available from the rotating type, which is at its best on a large lawn, to the oscillating bar, which is ideal for watering a small rectangular area thoroughly with no wastage. Watering is best done in the evening to minimize evaporation, and in a fine spray to give the water a chance to

drainage, resulting from compaction of the soil. Spiking the turf in autumn improves the drainage and also enables fertilizers to reach the grass roots, strengthening its growth and consequently ousting the moss. When spiking with a fork, there is no need to go deeper than 10 cm (4 in). The various sets of holes should be about 10 cm (4 in) apart all over the lawn. The ideal method of spiking a lawn is to use a special hollow-tined fork which removes cores of soil. If all this seems like too much hard work, you should be able to hire either a push or powered mechanical lawn aerator.

the soil is normal. If, however, the soil is clayey or badly compacted, mix the peat with an equal quantity of gritty sand and apply the top dressing at the rate of 1.5 kg per sq m (1½ lb per sq yd). Take care not to apply the dressing so thickly at any point that it smothers the grass. By making such annual dressings, it is possible to smooth out any small bumps and hollows and to greatly improve the quality of the lawn. If you have good supplies of your own compost, you can also make a superb lawn dressing by mixing equal quantities of sieved compost, soil and gritty sand.

(13) The texture of the soil in a lawn, whether it has been spiked or not, can be improved by an annual top dressing in autumn. A top dressing of peat can be applied at the rate of 0.5 kg per sq m (1 lb per sq yd) and brushed in, or worked in with the back of a rake, if

(14) A crumbling lawn edge can be repaired (autumn is the best time) by lifting a square of turf at the lawn edge and reversing it so that the broken edge is towards the centre of the lawn. The damaged area can then be filled with a mixture of soil and peat and, if necessary, resown. A similar measure, with a square of turf from a little used and seldom seen part of the lawn can be used to patch damage to a prominent area of the lawn. Swop the good area of turf for the damaged piece and resow as necessary.

soak in without forming puddles. If you decide to water during a dry spell, it is essential to ensure penetration of the water to a depth of 5 cm (2 in) if it is to do any good. Insufficient watering will harm the grass by encouraging shallow rooting. If the soil has become baked hard, it may be necessary to attempt to spike the lawn with a fork before you begin watering.

Even a lawn which has the clippings removed when it is cut tends to form a mat of dead foliage on the surface which resists the passage of air and water to grass roots. The name usually given to this matted grass is 'thatch'. In spring and autumn the dead matter should be removed from the lawn with a spring-tined rake, an operation called scarifying.

LAWN CALENDAR

Early spring	Scarify the grass with a spring-tined lawn rake, and cut the lawn when necessary.
Mid-spring	Apply a lawn fertilizer and increase the frequency of grass cutting.
Late spring	Inspect for weeds and apply a weedkiller if necessary.
Summer	Cut the grass at least once a week and water if necessary in the evenings. Persistent weeds such as yarrow may need a second application of weedkiller.
Early autumn	Take appropriate action to remove wormcasts and worms if necessary. Use a suitable autumn lawn fertilizer and reduce the frequency of mowing.
Mid-autumn	Scarify the grass with a spring-tined lawn rake. Spike all over with a fork and spread a top dressing.
Late autumn	Remove all fallen leaves.
Early winter	Keep off the grass if it is wet or frozen. Following a mild autumn you may have to give it a final cut of the year.
Mid-winter	Rake up the last of the previous autumn's leaves.
Late winter	Put down dry peat and sweep away worm casts.

If the lawn gets considerable use in the summer, the soil may have become compacted with the give-away sign of moss starting to flourish. The cure is to spike the lawn all over to a depth of 10 cm (4 in) with a garden fork. Then after spiking, improve the texture of the soil by applying a top dressing of peat, soil and sand. However, do not apply the dressing so thickly that it smothers the grass.

Feeding normally helps to avoid most lawn problems, but occasionally after a very wet winter or exceptionally dry summer moss can invade the lawn. You can either remove this by repeated raking and feeding, or you can kill the moss with a fertilizer containing sulphate of iron. But the cheapest way of killing moss is to use a special moss killer, watered on to the lawn.

Should your lawn develop uneven bumps—perhaps it is a lawn which you have just taken over—the answer is to lift the turf and to remove some of the soil from underneath. Conversely, hollows can be filled by lifting the turf and adding soil. Never roll a lawn. Rolling may be fine for bowling greens and cricket pitches, but it has no place in the garden.

A crumbling lawn edge can be repaired in autumn by lifting a square of turf at the lawn edge and reversing it so that the broken edge is towards the centre of the lawn.

Worms in lawns produce unsightly casts on the lawn in autumn and winter. The usual way of dealing with this problem is to scatter some dry peat on the lawn and then to brush this off together with the worm casts. In some areas moles can cause havoc on lawns in their search for worms. So you have a simple choice: either you kill the moles or use a proprietary wormkiller to remove the moles' source of food and also, incidentally, get rid of the wormcasts. The snag with this latter solution is that worms aerate the soil. So their removal inevitably means more work for the gardener in spiking the turf.

Weeds are the greatest problem with lawns. Selective weedkillers, either allied to fertilizers, or separately in liquid form (the cheapest and most effective method), will kill all lawn weeds when applied as instructed by the manufacturers. Weedkillers are most effective during showery weather between late spring and early autumn while the weeds are growing strongly. However they must not be used on lawns less than a year old. Similarly the clippings from a lawn treated with weedkiller must be composted for at least six months before they can be used as part of the compost. The alternative is to burn them.

Trees

Once you plant a tree in your garden, you have added something permanent. No wonder trees are so often chosen as living reminders of some happy event. Naturally with something which is going to be there for many years to come you have to give your choice careful thought.

The most important considerations in selecting a tree are the space available and the soil. For there are dozens of trees suitable for all sorts of positions, from dwarf trees suitable for back gardens to forest giants. There are trees which are not at all fussy about soil, while there are others with a marked preference for alkaline or acid conditions.

Trees can be chosen for the beauty of their leaves, their flowers or their fruit. You can also select a tree on account of its shape, be it columnar, round-headed or weeping. Some trees look good in isolation as single specimens on the lawn, while others, such as the birch, are at their best when planted in groups of three or four. It is vital to look ahead to the size and appearance of each tree in its maturity when making your selection.

Trees can give shelter from prevailing winds and provide shade in summer. However, do not plant a tree which will overshadow and grow to a size which will be out of proportion to your home. Most importantly, avoid planting vigorous or moisture-hungry trees such as the weeping willow or the poplar too close to the house, where their branches or roots may be a danger both to the building itself and to drains.

If you want to plant several trees, choose them both to contrast and complement one another—for instance, by mingling trees with red leaves with

Below: Prunus serrulata 'Kanzan'.
Right: Acer palmatum 'Senkaki', a maple.
Previous page: A fine Lawson's cypress.

those of green and by growing both deciduous and evergreen trees.

Deciduous trees may be planted from late autumn to early spring, provided that the soil is not frozen or waterlogged. Evergreen and coniferous trees, on the other hand, are best planted in early and mid-spring.

Here then are some suggestions to help you to

decide. Except for the holly, which is an evergreen, and the cotoneaster, a semi-evergreen, the first group are all deciduous. The height and spread of each tree after 20 years is given. The problem with most trees is that they lose their leaves in autumn and leave the garden with little in the way of interest over the dull winter period. The answer is to plant a few conifers or dwarf conifers.

ORNAMENTAL TREES

Almond (ornamental)

Attraction: Pink flowers in spring.
Soil: Any.
Size after 20 years: 6 m by 3m (20 ft by 10 ft)
Recommended species: *Prunus dulcis* (syn: *Amygdalus*)

Ash (Golden ash and Weeping ash)

Attraction: Beautiful foliage and pleasing shape.
Soil: Any.

Size after 20 years: Golden ash, 5 m by 3 m
(17 ft by 10 ft); Weeping ash, 3.6 m by 6m (12 ft by 20 ft)
Recommended species: *Fraxinus excelsior* 'Aurea' and
Fraxinus excelsior 'Pendula'.

Birch (Silver birch and Weeping birch)

Attraction: Silvery white bark and pendulous branches.
Soil: Any, including poor, light soil.
Size after 20 years: Silver birch, 7.5 m by 3 m
(25 ft by 10 ft); Weeping birch, 3.6 m by 3 m (12 ft by 10 ft).
Recommended species: *Betula pendula* (Silver birch) and
Betula pendula 'Youngii' (Young's weeping birch).

Catalpa (Indian bean tree)

Attraction: White, yellow and purple flowers are followed by brown seed pods. The leaves are large, yellow and heart-shaped.
Soil: Any.
Size after 20 years: 4.5 m by 3 m (15 ft by 10 ft).
Recommended species: *Catalpa bignonioides* 'Aurea'.

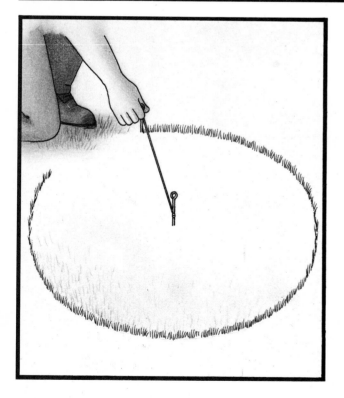

(1) Many trees are planted in grassed areas. So the first task is to remove a circle of turf a metre (yard) wide. This job can be done neatly by inserting a short stake in the centre of the intended circle with a piece of string attached to a second stick. The circumference of the circle can then be marked out.

(2) Skim away the turf from the marked out area with a spade and place it to one side. Next remove all of the soil from the hole to at least one spit and place in a garden barrow (or on a piece of thick plastic on the lawn). Then, using a fork, break up the subsoil thoroughly.

Cherry (ornamental)

Attraction: Blossom in spring, and autumn (depending on species).
Soil: Any, provided it is fairly well drained.
Size after 20 years: Varies considerably according to the species.
Recommended species:
Prunus 'Pandora' 4.5 m by 4.5 m (15 ft by 15 ft), pink flowers.
Prunus sargentii, 3.6 m by 4.5 m (12 ft by 15 ft), pink flowers.
Prunus subhirtella 'Autumnalis Rosea', 4.5 m by 4.5 m (15 ft by 15 ft), pink flower in autumn and winter.

Cotoneaster

Attraction: Semi-evergreen leaves and branches laden with red berries in autumn.
Soil: Any.
Size after 20 years: 4.5 m by 3.6 m (15 ft by 12 ft).
Recommended species: *Cotoneaster hybridus* 'Pendulus'.

Crab apple

Attraction: Flowers, followed in some species by fruit suitable for making jelly.
Soil: Any.
Size after 20 years: Varies considerably according to the species.
Recommended species:
Malus floribunda (Japanese Crab) 4.5 m by 3.6 m (15 ft by 12 ft), pink blossom followed by red fruit.
Malus 'John Downie', 6 m by 4.5 m (20 ft by 15 ft), white blossom followed by red and yellow fruit suitable for jelly.
Malus 'Red Jade', 3.6 m by 3.6 m (12 ft by 12 ft), pink flowers followed by red fruit.

False acacia

Attraction: Elegant foliage.
Soil: Any, including poor thin soils.
Size after 20 years: 6 m by 3.6 m (20 ft by 12 ft).
Recommended species: *Robinia pseudoacacia* 'Frisia'. The yellow leaves turn copper before falling in autumn.

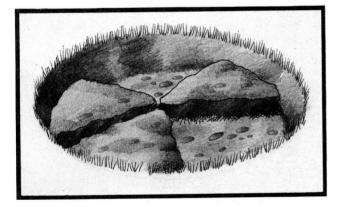

(3) Lay the pieces of turf face down at the foot of the hole.

(4) Examine the roots of the tree before planting and cut off any damaged pieces

cleanly with secateurs. Then place the tree in the hole, with the roots spread out, and check that the nursery soil level mark at the foot of the trunk corresponds with the soil level in your garden. If not, make the necessary soil level adjustments.

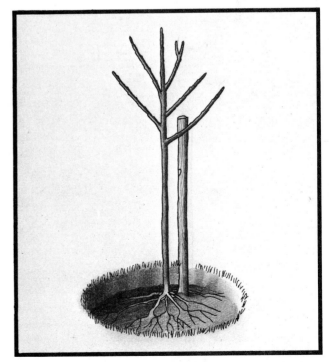

(5) Before filling in soil around the tree roots,

Hawthorn

Attraction: Superb blossom, followed by orange red berries.
Soil: Any.
Size after 20 years: 4.5 m by 3.6 m (15 ft by 12 ft)
Recommended species: *Crataegus × carrierei.*

Holly

Attraction: Glossy evergreen leaves and scarlet berries.
Soil: Any, provided well drained.
Size after 20 years: 6 m by 3.6 m (20 ft by 12 ft).
Recommended species: *Ilex aquifolium* 'J.C. van Tol'. Most hollies are either male or female; this one is self-fertile.

Honey locust

Attraction: Bright yellow leaves and twisted seed pods in autumn.
Soil: Any, tolerates drought.
Size after 20 years: 5.4 m by 2.4 m (18 ft by 8 ft).
Recommended species: *Gleditschia tricanthos* 'Sunburst'.

Japanese cherry

Attraction: Beautiful blossom in spring.
Soil: Any, provided it is fairly well drained.
Size after 20 years: Varies considerably according to the species.
Recommended species:
Prunus 'Amanogawa', 4.5 m by 1.2 m (15 ft by 4 ft), shell pink blossom. Ideal tree for a small garden or confined spaces.
Prunus 'Kanzan', 4.5 m by 4.5 m (15 ft by 15 ft), double rich pink flowers.
Prunus 'Pink Perfection', 3.6 m by 4.5 m (12 ft by 15 ft), rosy pink flowers.
Prunus 'Shirofugen', 4.5 m by 4.5 m (15 ft by 15 ft), pink flowers.
Prunus 'Tai Haku', 6 m by 6 m (20 ft by 20 ft), snow-white blossom in large pendulous clusters.

---

a sturdy stake of a suitable height should be inserted firmly in the bottom of the hole on the side from which the prevailing wind blows. The reason for doing this at this stage is to avoid damage later to the tree's roots.

(6) If your soil is of good quality, you can use it to fill in around the tree's roots. If not, it

is best to fill in with an equal mixture of soil and moist peat. As you fill in, tread the soil with your heel and give the trunk of the tree a gentle shake from time to time to settle the soil around its roots.

(7) The final and important task in planting is to secure the tree to the stake with a plastic or canvas tree-tie. The tree must be held firm without the trunk chaffing on the stake. If you are unable to get a proper tree-tie, use a nylon stocking looped around the stake and trunk in a figure of eight. Check the tree tie from time to time, especially after gales. As the tree grows it will, of course, be necessary to make adjustments to the tree tie.

Judas tree

Attraction: Clusters of rosy-purple flowers in late spring followed by purple-tinted seed pods in mid summer.
Soil: Good, well drained soil.
Size after 20 years: 4.5 m by 3 m (15 ft by 10 ft).
Recommended species: *Cercis siliquastrum.*

Laburnum (Golden Rain)

Attraction: Long racemes of golden-yellow flowers in late spring.
Soil: Ordinary, provided well drained.
Size after 20 years: 4.5 m by 3.6 m (15 ft by 12 ft).
Recommended species: *Laburnum × wateri* 'Vossii'. Fewer seed pods are produced than with other laburnums. All laburnum seed is very poisonous.

Maple

Attraction: Beautiful foliage and in some species colourful bark.
Soil: Ordinary and well drained. Japanese species need lime-free soil.
Size after 20 years: Varies considerably according to the species.
Recommended species:
Acer grosseri (Snake bark maple), 4.5 m by 4.5 m (15 ft by 15 ft).
Acer griseum (Paper bark maple), 3.6 m by 3.6 m (12 ft by 12 ft).
Acer Japonicum 'Aureum', 1.5 m by 1.5 m (5 ft by 5 ft), slow-growing with soft yellow leaves which turn crimson in fall.
Acer negundo 'Auratum', 6 m by 4.5 m (20 ft by 15 ft).
Acer palmatum 'Atropurpureum' (Purple Japanese Maple), 3.6 m by 3 m (12 ft by 10 ft).
Acer platanoides 'Royal Red' (Norway maple), 7.5 m by 4.5 m (25 ft by 15 ft).
Acer rubrum 'Zlesengeri' (Canadian red maple), 7.5 m by 5.4 m (25 ft by 18 ft).
Colours best in autumn on a lime-free soil.
Acer saccharinum (Silver maple), 7.5 m by 4.5 m (25 ft by 15 ft).

Maintain a weed-free circle of soil around the tree's trunk for several years until it is established as many trees die from the competition of grass roots for moisture.

a saw cut under the branch first. Then cut away the branch in small sections before you make the final saw cut downwards flush with the trunk. This procedure will remove the possibility of those nasty wounds inflicted on trees by a thoughtless saw cut which can result in the weight of the branch tearing it from the tree before the gardener has time to finish the job.

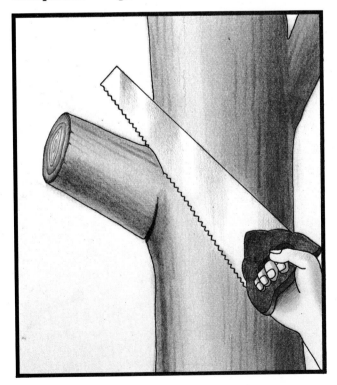

(8) If for some reason it becomes necessary to remove a large branch from a tree, make

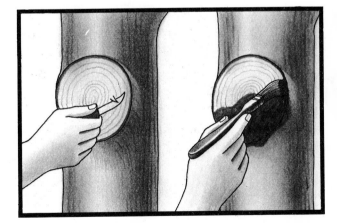

(9) When a branch has been cut away, the edges of the wound should be pared smooth with a sharp knife and then the wound painted over on a mild, dry day with a wound-sealing paint to prevent the entry of fungus or disease.

Mountain ash (Rowan)

Attraction: Leaf tints in autumn and abundance of berries.
Soil: Ordinary and well drained. Best results on acid soils.
Size after 20 years: 4.5 m by 3.6 m (15 ft by 12 ft).
Recommended species:
Sorbus aucuparia 'Carpet of Gold', golden yellow berries.
Sorbus aucuparia 'Sheerwater Seedling', orange red fruit.
Sorbus 'Joseph Rock', amber berries and leaves which turn to purple, burnt orange and copper.

Plum (ornamental)

Attraction: Deep purple leaves and pink flowers which open on the leafless branches in early spring.
Soil: Any.
Size after 20 years: 4.5 m by 4.5 m (15 ft by 15 ft).

Recommended species: *Prunus cerasifera* 'Nigra'.

Snowy mespilus (Shadbush)

Attraction: White flowers in mid spring when the half-opened leaves are tinged pink. Crimson fruit opens in early summer, and in autumn the foliage turns red and yellow.
Soil: Moist loam.
Size after 20 years: 6 m by 4.5 m (20 ft by 15 ft).
Recommended species: *Amelanchier canadensis*.

Willow (American weeping willow)

Attraction: Graceful umbrella of cascading branches.
Soil: Moist loam.
Size after 20 years: 3.6 m by 4.5 m (12 ft by 15 ft).
Recommended species: *Salix purpurea* 'Pendula'. This is the only weeping willow for average gardens. Golden forms all become much too large.

CONIFERS NOTE: any soil is suitable for these trees, except **Mountain Pine** (best on lime) and *Chamaecyparis pisifera* 'Boulevard' (needs lime-free soil).

Name	Size after 10 years (height by spread)	Foliage
CONIFERS FOR SMALL TO MEDIUM-SIZED GARDENS		
Cupressus		
Cupressus macrocarpa 'Donard Gold'	3 m by 90 cm (10 ft by 3 ft)	golden yellow
Juniper		
Juniperus communis 'Hibernica'	2.4 m by 60 cm (8 ft by 2 ft)	silvery green
Juniperus virginiana 'Skyrocket'	2.10 m by 39 cm (7 ft by 15 in)	blue-grey
Lawson's cypress		
Chamaecyparis lawsoniana 'Columnaris'	3 m by 60 cm (10 ft by 2 ft)	blue-green
'Ellwoodii'	1.8 m by 90 cm (6 ft by 3 ft)	blue-green
'Pembury Blue'	2.4 m by 60 cm (8 ft by 2 ft)	silver-blue
'Stewartii'	2.4 m by 1.2 m (8 ft by 4 ft)	yellowish green
Mountain Pine		
Pinus mugo	90 cm by 1.5 m (3 ft by 5 ft)	bright green
Spruce		
Picea pungens glauca 'Koster'	1.8 m by 60 cm (6 ft by 2 ft)	silver-blue
DWARF CONIFERS		
Juniper		
Juniperus communis 'Compressa'	38 cm by 15 cm (15 in by 6 in)	bluish grey
'Hornbrookii'	15 cm by 1.2 m (6 in by 4 ft)	green and bronze
Juniperus horizontalis 'Bar Harbor'	7.5 cm by 1.5 m (3 in by 5 ft)	grey-green
Lawson's cypress		
Chamaecyparis lawsoniana 'Minima Aurea'	38 cm by 25 cm (15 in by 10 in)	gold
Chamaecyparis pisifera 'Boulevard'	1.2 m by 60 cm (4 ft by 2 ft)	silver blue
Spruce		
Picea glauca albertiana 'Conica'	60 cm by 25 cm (2 ft by 10 in)	bright green
Western red cedar		
Thuja occidentalis 'Rheingold'	1.2 m by 90 cm (4 ft by 3 ft)	bronze and gold

Shrubs & Climbers

Shrubs give a garden its character. With a suitable choice you can have colour all year round as well as many interesting shapes and contrasts. Shrubs, unlike many other garden plants, have a long life and, once established, require little attention while they increase in size and beauty with the passing years.

There are large shrubs and tiny shrubs and shrubs which need walls and fences for support. There are shrubs for all seasons and to suit all tastes. With the right sort of shrubs in your garden, it need never be dull. However, with such a large choice of shrubs, it can be difficult to decide on the ones most suitable for your particular garden. The tables below give a selection of some of those shrubs particularly suitable for certain conditions or with a particular attraction. The most important considerations in making a choice are generally soil, site, temperatures and local weather conditions.

Most shrubs are fortunately indifferent to the alkalinity or acidity of the soil within the limits found in the majority of gardens. There is a group of shrubs, however, which are known as lime-hating

or calcifuge, including the camellias, rhododendrons and most of the heathers. When the soil is alkaline, these shrubs are unable to take up certain essential minerals, mainly iron, with the result that they become sickly and suffer from chlorosis, a yellowing of the leaves. The addition of peat and compost to lime soils will gradually make them more acid and consequently more suited to calcifuge plants. But if your soil is distinctly alkaline you will be fighting a losing battle and it is advisable to stick to the majority of shrubs— and there are some splendid ones among them—

SHRUBS SUITABLE FOR CHALKY OR ALKALINE SOILS

DECIDUOUS

Berberis (Barberry)
Buddleia
Chaenomeles (Japanese quince or Japonica)
Clematis
Clerodendron
Cotoneaster
Daphne
Deutzia
Forsythia
Hypericum calycinum (Rose of Sharon)
Potentilla (Shrubby cinquefoil)
Rhus (Sumach)
Ribes (Flowering currant)
Rubus (Bramble)
Spiraea
Symphoricarpos (Snowberry)
Syringa (Lilac)
Viburnum

EVERGREEN

Berberis (Barberry)
Choisya (Mexican orange blossom)
Escallonia
Hebe (Veronica)
Hypericum calycinum (Rose of Sharon)
Ilex (Holly)
Laurus (Sweet bay, Bay laurel)
Viburnum
Yucca (Adam's needle or Candle of the Lord)

SHRUBS SUITABLE FOR NEUTRAL TO SLIGHTLY ACID CLAY SOILS

DECIDUOUS

Abelia
Berberis (Barberry)
Chaenomeles (Japanese quince or Japonica)
Colutea (Bladder senna)
Cornus (Dogwood)
Corylus (Hazel)
Cotinus (Smoke bush)
Cotoneaster
Cytisus (Broom)
Forsythia
Genista (Broom)
Hamamelis (Witch hazel)
Hibiscus
Lonicera (Honeysuckle)
Magnolia
Philadelphus (Mock orange)
Ribes (Flowering currant)
Rosa (Rose)
Spiraea
Symphoricarpos (Snowberry)
Weigela

EVERGREEN

Aucuba
Berberis (Barberry)
Choisya (Mexican orange blossom)
Cotoneaster
Lonicera (Honeysuckle)
Mahonia
Magnolia
Osmanthus
Pyracantha (Firethorn)
Rhododendron
Senecio
Skimmia

which like alkaline conditions.

Getting the right shrubs to suit your soil is of course only half the battle. The other aspect is climate. The majority of evergreens, for example, like plenty of moisture. If you wish to grow such shrubs in drier, colder areas, frequent watering and regular mulching will be vital to keep the shrubs healthy. Young evergreen shrubs too are likely to need protection in winter until established.

A key factor with most shrubs is the amount

of cold they can endure. The ability of a shrub to resist cold depends partly on the soil and the site. The floor of a sheltered valley is not the ideal place to grow tender shrubs as cold air runs downhill like water and the lower hollows become pockets for frost and chilling damp fog and mist patches. Freezing winds are more damaging than low temperature, and if the shoots become well ripened, they will withstand more cold than the soft, sappy growth made in dull wet positions. Wet, heavy soil and too much nitrogen fertilizer also encourage the wrong sort of weak growth, whereas well-drained soils, rich in potash help to ensure strong, healthy shrubs.

Apart from the weather, another hazard which faces gardeners in some areas is atmospheric pollution from traffic or local industries. The worst of the noxious gases is sulphur dioxide. Some

SHRUBS SUITABLE FOR DRY ACID SOILS

DECIDUOUS

Berberis (Barberry)
Colutea (Bladder senna)
Cotoneaster
Genista (Broom)
Indigofera
Kerria (Batchelor's buttons)
Lonicera (Honeysuckle)
Salix repens (Creeping willow)
Tamarix (Tamarisk)

EVERGREEN

Berberis (Barberry)
Calluna (Ling or Heather)
Cistus (Rock rose)
Cotoneaster
Elaeagnus (Oleaster)
Erica (Heather)
Ilex crenata (Japanese holly)
Juniperus (Juniper)
Lonicera (Honeysuckle)
Pernettya (Chilean pernettya)

SHRUBS SUITABLE FOR WET DISTRICTS AND MOIST GROUND

DECIDUOUS

Amelanchier canadensis (Shadbush, June berry or Snowy mespilus)
Cornus alba and *stonifera* varieties (Dogwood)
Hippophae (Sea buckthorn)
Hydrangea —not Hortensia varieties
Philadelphus (Mock orange)
Salix (Willow)
Sambucus (Elder)
Spiraea × *bumalda* 'Anthony Waterer'
Viburnum opulus
Weigela

SHRUBS SUITABLE FOR HOT AND DRY POSITIONS

DECIDUOUS

Berberis (Barberry)
Caryopteris (Bluebeard)
Chaenomeles (Japanese or quince or Japonica)
Colutea (Bladder senna)
Cotinus (Smoke bush)
Cytisus (Broom)
Genista (Broom)
Hedysarum
Hippophae (Sea buckthorn)
Indigofera
Perovskia (Russian sage)
Potentilla (Shrubby cinquefoil)
Rhus (Sumach)
Robinia (Acacia)
Rosa spinosissima hybrids
Rubus (Bramble)
Spartium (Spanish broom)
Spiraea
Tamarix (Tamarisk)

EVERGREEN

Artemisia abrotanum (Southernwood or Lad's love)
Artiplex (Tree purselane)
Berberis (Barberry)
Buxus (Box)
Cistus (Rock rose)
Cotoneaster low varieties
Euonymus fortunei varieties (Winter creeper)
Hebe (Veronica)
Hedera (Ivy)
Helichrysum
Hypericum calycinum (Rose of Sharon)
Juniperus—low varieties—(Juniper)
Lavandula (Lavender)
Olearia (Daisy bush)
Phlomis (Jerusalem sage)
Rosemarinus (Rosemary)
Santolina (Cotton lavender)
Senecio
Ulex (Gorse, Furge or Whin)
Vinca (Periwinkle)
Yucca (Adam's needle or Candle of the Lord)

evergreens become deciduous or partly so; some become stunted, while others may flower late or not at all.

Yet shrubs are remarkably resilient. Roses, for example, thrive even in the busiest industrial cities, and indeed the atmospheric pollution may even have the effect of acting like a fungicide in helping them to avoid such a debilitating disease as blackspot. Roses, in fact, grow better in urban areas than, say, by the sea, which helps towards their enormous popularity.

It is not commonly appreciated how useful shrubs are in providing a labour-saving garden. One of the least pleasant tasks in the garden, for instance, is keeping down the weeds. Hoeing might be a means of gentle relaxation, and the use of weedkillers quick and simple. But if you have more important things to do with your time let the shrubs do the weeding for you. What actually happens is that ground-hugging shrubs are planted under and between the taller shrubs to smother any weed seedlings that may attempt to grow.

Ground cover shrubs, as they are collectively known, make a vast improvement to the look of any garden. With deciduous shrubs you are often left with unattractive areas of bare soil between late autumn and mid-spring, but by surrounding them with such beauties as *Euonymous fortunei* 'Emerald 'n' Gold' and *Cotoneaster salicifolius* 'Autumn Fire', even on the bleakest days your garden will delight the eye. After the initial cost, and once the ground cover shrubs themselves are well

---

SHRUBS SUITABLE FOR COLD WINDSWEPT AREAS

DECIDUOUS

Cornus (Dogwood)
Cotinus (Smoke bush)
Hippophae (Sea buckthorn)
Hydrangea paniculata 'Grandiflora'
Kerria (Batchelor's buttons)
Philadelphus (Mock orange)
Salix (Willow)
Spiraea
Tamarix (Tamarisk)
Viburnum opulus varieties

EVERGREEN

Calluna (Ling or Heather)
Chamaecyparis lawsoniana obtusa 'Pygmea'
  (Dwarf Lawson's cypress)
Elaeagnus (Oleaster)
Euonymus fortunei varieties (Winter creeper)
Gaultheria (Checkerberry)
Juniperus communis varieties (Juniper)
Mahonia aquifolium (Oregon holly grape)
Pachysandra (Japanese spurge)
Pernettya (Chilean pernettya)
Thuja occidentalis varieties (Arbor-vitae)
Ulex (Gorse, Furge or Whin)

SHRUBS SUITABLE FOR SHADY AND SUNLESS POSITIONS

DECIDUOUS

Acer palmatum (Maple)★
Chaenomeles (Japanese quince or Japonica)
Cornus alba (Dogwood)
Daphne★
Hypericum calycinum (Rose of Sharon)★
Jasminum nudiflorum (Winter flowering jasmine)
Kerria (Batchelor's buttons)
Leycesteria (Flowering nutmeg)
Lonicera periclymenum (Honeysuckle)
Ribes (Flowering currant)★
Sambucus (Elder)★
Spiraea × bumulda 'Anthony Waterer'
Symphoricarpos (Snowberry)★
Viburnum winter flowering varieties★

> ★suitable for planting under trees

EVERGREEN

Aucuba★
Buxus (Box)★
Camellia★
Choisya (Mexican orange blossom)
Cotoneaster low varieties★
Danae★
Euonymus fortunei varieties (Winter creeper)★
Garrya (Silk tassel bush or California catkin bush)
Gaultheria (Checkerberry)★
Hedera (Ivy)★
Hypericum calycinum (Rose of Sharon)★
Juniperus × media 'Pfitzerana' (Juniper)
Laurus (Sweet bay or Bay laurel)
Ligustrum (Privet)★
Mahonia★
Olearia (Daisy bush)
Pachysandra (Japanese spurge)★
Pernettya (Chilean pernettya)★
Phillyrea★
Pyracantha (Firethorn)
Rhododendron dwarf species★
Ruscus (Butcher's broom)★
Sarcococca (Christmas box)★
Skimmia★
Viburnum winter flowering varieties★

> ★suitable for planting under trees

established, the shrub beds will require the minimum of maintenance.

However, a word of warning: even the best ground cover shrubs will be useless in combating perennial weeds such as bindweed, couch grass, dandelions, docks and ground elder. These particular weeds must be eliminated before you do any planting at all. Also when you use ground cover shrubs, the soil has extra demands placed on it initially in the way of providing extra plant foods. So help out by feeding annually in spring with a granular general fertilizer at least until the shrubs are sufficiently large to need no further encouragement to produce further growth.

Thousands of years ago the Romans and Greeks did much of their growing of shrubs in urns and other decorative containers, which lined the formal gardens of large villas, palaces and temples. With today's smaller gardens many beautiful shrubs can be grown in a similar way and stood on paved areas. The root restriction of the container incidentally often produces unexpected benefits such as more flowers.

Shrubs not more than 30 cm (1 ft) tall can be grown happily in window boxes and troughs, measuring at least 30 cm wide by 30 cm deep

---

SHRUBS SUITABLE FOR INDUSTRIAL AREAS

DECIMUS

Amelanchier canadensis (Shadbush, June berry or snowy mespilus)
Berberis (Barberry)
Ceanothus (Californian lilac)
Chaenomeles (Japanese quince or Japonica)
Clethra (Sweet pepper)
Cotoneaster
Deutzia
Forsythia
Hydrangea macrophylla Lacecap varieties
Hypericum calycinum (Rose of Sharon)
Kerria (Batchelor's buttons)
Parthenocissus (Virginia creeper)
Philadelphus (Mock orange)
Rhus typhina (Stag's Horn Sumach)
Ribes (Flowering currant)
Rosa (Rose)
Spiraea
Symphoricarpos (Snowberry)
Syringa (Lilac)
Viburnum
Weigela

EVERGREEN

Arbutus (Strawberry tree)
Berberis (Barberry)
Buxus (Box)
Cotoneaster
Elaeagnus (Oleaster)
Euonymus fortunei varieties (Winter creeper)
Hedera (Ivy)
Hypericum calycinum (Rose of Sharon)
Ilex (Holly)
Ligustrum (Privet)
Mahonia
Olearia (Daisy bush)
Osmanthus
Pyracantha (Firethorn)
Rhododendron
Sarcococca (Christmas box)
Senecio
Ulex (Gorse, Furge or Whin)
Viburnum
Vinca (Periwinkle)

SHRUBS SUITABLE FOR COASTAL OR SEASIDE AREAS

DECIDUOUS

Buddleia
Berberis (Barberry)
Colutea (Bladder senna)
Cotoneaster
Cytisus (Broom)
Fuchsia
Genista (Broom)
Hippophae (Sea buckthorn)
Hydrangea macrophylla Hortensia varieties
Rosa (Rose)
Sambucus (Elder)
Spartium (Spanish broom)
Spiraea
Symphoricarpos (Snowberry)
Viburnum

EVERGREEN

Artiplex (Tree purselane)
Arbutus (Strawberry tree)
Berberis (Barberry)
Cotoneaster
Elaeagnus pungens (Oleaster)
Erica arborea 'Alpina' (Tree heath)
Escallonia
Euonymus fortunei varieties (Winter creeper)
Griselinia
Helichrysum
Lavandula (Lavender)
Olearia (Daisy bush)
Phlomis (Jerusalem sage)
Pinus mugo (Mountain pine)
Pittosporum
Rosmarinus (Rosemary)
Senecio
Ulex (Gorse, Furge or Whin)
Viburnum

Right: Jasminum nudiflorum, one of the best known of winter flowering shrubs.

(1 ft by 1 ft) by a satisfactory length. However, larger shrubs, measuring as much as 1.5 m by 90 cm wide (5 ft by 3 ft) will need containers at least 60 cm wide by 45 cm deep (2 ft by 1½ ft) for healthy growth and also if the problem of constant watering is to be avoided.

The most common reason for planting shrubs in containers is shortage of space. Yet often little thought is given to making walls and fences into a home for shrubs and climbers. These make attractive features on house walls and they can be

SHRUBS SUITABLE FOR GROUND COVER

DECIDUOUS

Ceratostigma (Hardy plumbago)†
Cytisus (Broom)—low varieties†
Genista (Broom)†
Potentilla (Shrubby cinquefoil)†
Salix (Willow)★
Symphoricarpos (Snowberry)★†

★thrives well in shade or partial shade
†grows well in full sun

EVERGREEN

Berberis (Barberry)★†
Cistus (Rock rose)†
Cotoneaster★†
Erica (Heather)†
Euonymus fortunei (Winter creeper)★†
Gaultheria (Checkerberry)★†
Hebe (Veronica)★†
Hedera (Ivy)★†
Hypericum calycinum (Rose of Sharon)★†
Juniperus (Juniper)★†
Lavandula (Lavender)†
Mahonia★†
Pachysandra (Japanese spurge)★
Phlomis (Jerusalem sage)†
Ruta (Rue)†
Santolina (Cotton lavender)†
Sarcococca (Christmas box)★†
Viburnum davidii★
Vinca★

★thrives in shade or partial shade
†grows well in full sun

used to camouflage bare walls of garages and fences and to conceal dustbin areas.

The flowering season of many shrubs may last for a brief two weeks at most. Once the show is over there may be little to compensate for the loss of flowers and scent. There are fortunately a great number of shrubs with particularly pleasing foliage which will brighten your garden throughout the year. Some shrubs have red, purple or copper leaves when young which rival flowers for their appeal. *Pieris* 'Forest Flame', for instance, has bright red young leaves in late spring which are just as attractive as the bracts on the showy Mediterranean climber, the bougainvillea. Later the foliage turns through pink and creamy white to glossy green. The

41

SHRUBS SUITABLE FOR GROWING IN CONTAINERS

DECIDUOUS

Berberis (Barberry)
Clematis
Deutzia
Jasminum (Jasmine)
Lonicera (Honeysuckle)
Passiflora (Passion flower)
Prunus
Ribes (Flowering currant)
Spiraea
Syringa (Lilac)
Tamarix (Tamarisk)
Vitis (Vine)
Weigela

EVERGREEN

Aucuba
Berberis (Barberry)

Camellia
Chamaecyparis (False cypress)—dwarf varieties
Choisya (Mexican orange blossom)
Cistus (Rock rose)
Cotoneaster—smaller varieties
Euonymus fortunei (Winter creeper)
Hebe (Veronica)
Hypericum calycinum (Rose of Sharon)
Juniperus (Juniper)—dwarf varieties
Kerria
Laurus (Sweet bay or Bay laurel)
Lavandula (Lavender)
Lonicera (Honeysuckle)
Mahonia
Pernettya (Chilean pernettya)
Picea (Spruce)—dwarf varieties
Pinus (Pine)—dwarf varieties
Prunus
Pyracantha (Firethorn)
Rhododendron and *azalea*—dwarf varieties
Rosmarinus (Rosemary)

(1) Make the hole for the shrub as deep, but slightly wider than the shrub's original root ball. With a shrub in a container, the surface of the potting mixture in the container should be level with that of the surrounding soil. With a bare or balled-root shrub, the mark on the stem, showing the soil level at the nursery, should correspond to the level of the soil in your garden. If you are planting a large shrub, or a shrub in its own bed on the lawn, it may be necessary to break up the subsoil with a fork and to work in some peat or some garden compost (see illustration 2, page 30).

(2) Gently ease the shrub from its container before placing it in the hole. If the container is made of polythene, slit it first with a knife. The hessian around balled-root shrubs should not be eased away until the shrub is sitting snugly in the hole. With bare-root shrubs, check that none of the roots is damaged. Damaged pieces of root can be trimmed off cleanly with secateurs before the roots are well spread out in the hole.

Some young shrubs, such as magnolias and lilacs, need stakes to prevent their rocking from side to side and so damaging the root system. The main stem should be secured to most useful shrubs for foliage effect are those with coloured leaves during the entire growing season, or, in the case of evergreens, all year. There are many such shrubs in shades of red, yellow, grey and silver and numerous variegated combinations.

Before any shrub or climber can be planted, the soil has to be properly prepared. If you have a new garden, or a neglected one, you should fork out every last piece of any of the persistent perennial weeds. Should you have a large area to clear, your best plan is to use one of the modern chemical weedkillers which will avoid the possibility of problems later—problems such as bindweed around the roots and stems of a treasured shrub.

In most gardens it will be enough to dig over the soil to one spit's depth in autumn or winter in the normal way. If the soil is poor, it may be necessary to incorporate at the same time considerable quantities of farmyard manure, garden compost or peat into the shrub bed. It is worth remembering that organic material is the life blood of your soil and that without it the benefits of chemical fertilizers are largely lost. However, if the soil is fairly fertile, it should be sufficient to incorporate the compost or peat in the soil around the roots of the individual shrub at planting time.

It used to be the rule that deciduous shrubs were planted any time between late autumn and early spring, provided that the soil was not waterlogged or frozen over. One was advised to plant evergreens in early autumn or spring. Such advice still holds good if you are sufficiently organized to take advantage of the traditional planting times. However, with garden centres today selling shrubs in containers you can plant at almost any time of the year.

Shrubs are supplied by nurseries in three ways: with bare roots; with balled roots; or in a plastic pot, containing potting mixture. Balled-root shrubs, particularly conifers and rhododendrons, have some soil around their roots kept in place by a piece of hessian. The intention is to keep the

a stake, inserted in the hole close to the stem of the shrub before you fill in with soil to avoid unnecessary damage to the roots (see illustrations 5 and 7, pages 31-2).

(3) Fill in carefully around the roots with good soil or a mixture of moist peat and soil. The peat is especially beneficial if you are planting a shrub which is known to like acid soil conditions. If the shrub was supplied in bare-root form, give it a gentle shake from time to time to make sure that it is well settled. Provided the soil is not too heavy or wet, firm it with your heel or fingers around the base of the shrub. Depending on the time of year and the weather, it may be necessary to water thoroughly.

(4) Planting a shrub against a wall or fence calls for some special care as the soil in such positions is frequently poor and dries out quickly. So make the planting hole about twice as large as is actually necessary and fork some compost into the bottom.

SHRUBS AND CLIMBERS SUITABLE FOR WALLS AND FENCES

DECIDUOUS

Abelia
Actinidia★
Akebia★
Aristolochia (Dutchman's pipe)★
Buddleia
Campsis (Trumpet vine)
Celastrus (Climbing bittersweet or Staff vine)
Chaenomeles (Japanese quince or Japonica)
Chimonathus (Winter sweet)
Clematis
Cotoneaster
Cytisus battandieri (Moroccan broom)
Fremontodendron
Fuchsia
Hebe hulkeana (Veronica)
Hydrangea petiolaris
Jasminum (Jasmine)★
Kerria
Lippia (Lemon scented verbena)
Lonicera (Honeysuckle)★
Parthenocissus (Virginia creeper)
Passiflora (Passion flower)
Polygonum (Russian vine or Mile-a-minute vine)
Prunus tribola 'Multiplex' (Dwarf Chinese almond)

Robina (Acacia)
Rosa (Rose)★
Vitis (Vine)★
Wisteria★

★can be used for training around poles and pergolas as well as on walls and fences

EVERGREEN

Cotoneaster
Escallonia
Garrya (Silk tassel bush or Californian catkin bush)
Hedera (Ivy)
Itea
Leptospermum
Lonicera (Honeysuckle)★
Magnolia grandiflora (Tree magnolia)
Myrtus (Myrtle)
Piptanthus
Pyracantha (Firethorn)
Raphiolepis
Solanum (Chilean potato tree)★

★can be used for training around poles and pergolas as well as on walls and fences

or wall shrub with good soil from another part of the garden or a mixture of soil and peat or compost.

(5) Climbers should be put into the hole so that their main stem is about 23 cm (9 in) out from the wall. With shrubs, the distance from the wall will depend on whether you wish to train the shrub against the wall or merely to use it as a means of providing shelter. Fill in around the roots of the climber

(6) The branches of most climbers are too short and too delicate to be trained immediately on to wires or trellis. So initially it is best to tie them loosely to a bamboo cane for support.

root system intact during transit so that the shrub will become established quickly once it is planted. Shrubs supplied in bare root form are restricted to those which transplant and become established easily. In general they are deciduous; the most common being roses, which are normally sold in this way. The snag, of course, with bare root shrubs is that you are limited to planting them in the dormant period. If you are buying a shrub container-grown at a garden centre, pick it up and check that it has a well-developed root system.

Spacing is a key consideration. It is always

SHRUBS WITH FRAGRANT FLOWERS

DECIDUOUS

Abelia
Akebia
Buddleia davidii varieties
Chimonanthus praecox (Winter sweet)
Clethra (Sweet pepper)
Daphne
Fothergilla
Hamamelis (Witch hazel)
Hoheria (New Zealand lace bark)
Jasminum officinale (Jasmine)
Lonicera periclymenum (Honeysuckle)
Philadelphus (Mock orange)—most
Poncirus (Hardy orange)
Rhododendron—many, but particularly the deciduous azaleas

Rosa (Rose)
Syringa (Lilac)
Viburnum—many
Wisteria

EVERGREEN

Choisya (Mexican orange blossom)
Corokia
Itea
Magnolia grandiflora (Tree magnolia)
Mahonia 'Charity'
Myrtus communis (Myrtle)
Osmanthus
Pillyrea
Rhododendron—many, but particularly the deciduous azaleas
Ulex (Gorse, Furge or Whin)
Viburnum—many

(7) Ivy, Virginia creeper and the climbing Hydrangea petiolaris are capable of clinging to walls without assistance. However, the majority of so-called 'climbers' need some sort of support. Wires are best attached to walls and fences with pieces of ironmongery called 'vine-eyes'. The spacing of the wires will be determined by the area you wish to cover and also whether you are training a climber or a wall shrub.

(8) For clematis and the modern recurrent flowering roses, trellis panels of plastic, metal or wood are ideal. The trellis should be firmly secured to plugs in the wall so that the support stands out about 3 cm (1 in) from the surface to make tying easier. Fasten the shoots of the climber loosely to the support with raffia or twine. A slight amount of free movement will ensure that delicate shoots are not broken by the wind.

45

tempting to plant the 'small' shrubs from the nursery much too close together. The general rule is that the space between shrubs should be about

SHRUBS BEARING AUTUMN BERRIES AND FRUIT

DECIDUOUS

Actinidia chinensis
Akebia quinata
Berberis (Barberry)
Callicarpa
Chaenomeles (Japanese quince or Japonica)
Celastrus (Climbing bittersweet or Staff vine)
Colutea (Bladder senna)
Cornus mas (Dogwood)
Cotoneaster
Euonymus alata (Winged spindle tree)
Hippophae rhamnoides (Sea buckthorn)
Passiflora caerulea (Passion flower)
Poncirus trifoliata (Hardy orange)
Punica (Pomegranate)
Rosa moyesii (Rose)
Staphylea (Bladder nut)
Symphoricarpos (Snowberry)
Vitis vinifera 'Brandt' (Vine)

EVERGREEN

Arbutus unedo (Strawberry tree)
Berberis (Barberry)
Cotoneaster
Gaultheria procumbens (Checkerberry)
Ilex aquifolium 'J. C. van Tol'
Mahonia aquifolium (Oregon holly grape)
Pernettya mucronata (Chilean pernettya)
Pyracantha (Firehorn)
Skimmia
Stranvaesia

SHRUBS AND CLIMBERS WITH FLOWERS AND/OR COLOURFUL STEMS FOR WINTER DISPLAY

DECIDUOUS

Chimonanthus (Winter sweet)
Cornus alba sibirica 'Westonbirt'
Corylus avellana 'Contorta'
Daphne mezereum
Hamamelis mollis (Witch hazel)
Jasminum nudiflorum (Jasmine)
Parrotia persica
Rosa sericea (Rose)
Stachyurus praecox
Viburnum × bodnantense 'Dawn'

EVERGREEN

Arbutus unedo (Strawberry tree)
Erica carnea (Winter or mountain heath, heather)
Erica × darleyensis (Darley Dale heath, heather)
Garrya elliptica (Californian catkin bush or Silk tassel bush)
Lonicera frangrantissima (Honeysuckle)
Mahonia 'Charity'
Rhododendron 'Praecox'
Sarcococca humilis (Christmas box)
Viburnum tinus 'Eve Price'

SHRUBS WITH ATTRACTIVE FOLIAGE

DECIDUOUS

Acer japonicum 'Aureum' (Maple)
Acer palmatum 'Atropurpureum' (Maple)
Actinidia kolomikta
Berberis thunbergii 'Atropurpurea' (Barberry)
Cornus alba sibirica 'Elegantissima' (Dogwood)
Corylus maxima 'Purpurea' (Ornamental hazel)
Cotinus coggyria 'Royal Purple' (Smoke bush)
Cytisus battandieri (Broom)
Fothergilla
Hippophae rhamnoides (Sea buckthorn)
Parrotia
Perovskia × 'Blue Spire' (Russian Sage)
Rhus typhina (Sumach)
Salix repens argentea (Creeping willow)
Sambucus racemosa 'Plumosa Aurea' (Elder)

EVERGREEN

Aucuba japonica 'Variegata'
Calluna vulgaris 'Gold Haze' (Ling or heather)
Cistus 'Silver Pink' (Rock rose)
Elaeagnus pungens 'Maculata' (Oleaster)
Euonymus fortunei 'Emerald 'n' Gold' (Winter creeper)
Hebe pinguifolia Pagei (Veronica)
Hypericum × moserianum 'Tricolour'
Ilex × altraclarensis 'Golden King' (Holly)
Lonicera nitida 'Baggessen's Gold' (Honeysuckle)
Photina × fraseri 'Robin Hood'
Pieris 'Forest Flame' (Lily-of-the valley tree)
Pittosporum tenuifolium 'Silver Queen'
Santolina neapolitana (Cotton lavender)
Senecio laxifolius
Vinca minor 'Variegata' (Periwinkle)

half the total of their ultimate spread. So if two shrubs are expected to spread 1 m (3 ft) and 1.5 m (4½ ft), you should plant them 1.25 m (3¾ ft) apart.

When planting, the soil should not be excessively wet, covered in snow or frozen over. If conditions are unsuitable, the shrubs are best kept in an unheated shed or garage until the weather improves. Do not take newly purchased shrubs into the warmth of your home, because when you put them outdoors again the shock will kill them. If bare-foot shrubs such as roses have to be kept for any length of time before they can be planted, cover their roots with some damp sacking or straw and soak the roots in a bucket of water overnight before planting. The alternative, if a spell of very wet weather sets in after you take delivery of your

(9) If a large shrub urgently needs staking (perhaps after a spell of windy weather), surround the shrub with three sturdy bamboo canes and secure some of the branches to each cane with twine. This takes the strain off the shrub's root system and helps it to recover. After a few months it may be possible to abandon this temporary support.

(11) The easiest way to protect an evergreen shrub in the open garden is to cover it with a white plastic sack with the bottom slit open. All you have to do is to surround the shrub with three or four suitably placed stakes. Then simply slip the plastic sack over the top. Why white plastic? Because it reflects the sunlight and does not overheat in winter.

(10) Wall shrubs and climbers can be protected from the ravages of winter wind and frost by mats made of straw or bracken woven into sheets of wire netting. The mats can then be held around the shrubs in a semicircle by means of bamboo canes.

(12) The most common way of protecting shrubs is to shield them on the windward side with a semicircle of sacking held between stakes. If you cannot get hessian, then polythene sheet in a suitably heavy thickness makes a satisfactory substitute.

47

roses, is to plant them still bunched together in an empty patch of soil in the vegetable plot until the soil in the rose bed becomes suitable for planting.

Shrubs are expensive. So once you have planted them it is important to ensure that they become established quickly and continue to thrive. The main requirement is water. It is easy to forget to water newly planted shrubs during the first spring and summer until it is too late.

The best way of conserving soil moisture and keeping the roots cool is to put down a layer of

(13) Shrubs which generally produce their new shoots from the base, either at or below ground level, such as Caryopteris, Cerato-stigma, Fuchsia and Perovskia, can be protected in this vital area by putting a 23 cm (9 in) layer of weathered ashes, coarse sand, bracken, straw or dry peat over them in late autumn. The protective layer should be removed when growth begins in spring.

(14) The best way of keeping the soil moist and free from weeds is to put down a mulch of compost, leaf-mould, spent hops, peat or shredded bark. Whatever material you

choose, make sure that the soil is moist before you spread the mulch, which should be at least 5 cm (2 in) thick. The mulch should be renewed each year in mid-spring.

(15) If the growth of a shrub is slower than expected, you can feed it with a granular general fertilizer at the rate of 135 gm per sq m (4 oz per sq yd) under the spread of the branches in spring before you apply the annual mulch. Rake it in.

(16) When planting a shrub in a container, the first essential is that, whatever type of

48

mulch. Whatever material you choose—garden compost, spent hops, leaf-mould, bracken, peat or shredded bark—make sure that the soil is moist before you put down the mulch, which should be at least 5 cm (2 in) thick if it is to do any good. If you use peat, remember to soak it thoroughly before you put it on the soil, as peat applied dry is almost completely water repellant.

All mulches are gradually absorbed into the soil, thus helping to improve its physical structure. But often they do little in the way of replenishing the soil's reserve of plant foods. If your shrubs fail

container you choose, it should have sufficient drainage holes in its base. If necessary, the container can be stood on a platform of bricks to ensure proper drainage. The next task is to put 3 to 5 cm (1 to 2 in) of drainage material, such as gravel or broken clay pots, in the bottom of the container. Then add a suitable proprietary potting mixture. That is one of the main advantages of container gardening: you can suit the soil exactly to a particular shrub.

(17) **Before planting, gently unwind some of the shrub's roots from the restriction placed on them by the nursery container, and trim off any damaged pieces. Then plant the shrub in the container so that the base of its stem is positioned about 3 cm (1 in) below the rim.**

(18) **Fill in with compost, firming with your**

fingers or a piece of wood, and water thoroughly. If the shrub is known to prefer acid conditions, use the rainwater whenever possible: your tap water may well be alkaline, even if you live in an area where your soil tests indicate that the soil is acid. A year after planting, feed a couple of times in summer with a liquid general fertilizer.

(19) **If your shrub grows too large, its growth can be limited by removing it from its container in early spring and pruning back the roots by 10 cm (4 in) before repotting the shrub with fresh mixture. Shrubs in containers can also have their branches pruned in the same way as shrubs growing in the normal way in the garden (see chapter 6), but the rule is never to do any more pruning than necessary; otherwise you may encourage the additional vigorous growth you wish to avoid.**

to make the sort of growth which is expected of them, feeding may be necessary. You can make a soil test to find out exactly what is required. or simply top dress the soil with a granular general fertilizer in spring just before you apply the annual mulch.

SHRUB CHECK LIST

PROBLEM	POSSIBLE CAUSE	REMEDY
Shrub looks sickly a few weeks after planting.	Faulty planting.	Lift the shrub and untangle the roots. Then replant at the correct depth with some moist compost and water copiously.
Flower buds fall off prematurely.	Frost or drought.	Give frost protection. Apply a mulch around the root area and water well during dry spells, particularly when the flower buds are forming.
Leaves have become mottled or turning yellow.	Chlorosis due to excessive lime in the soil.	Apply sequestered iron around the root area and mulch with moist peat. Better still, make a soil test and if too much lime is present, move the shrub to a more suitable position.
Failure to flower and perhaps accompanied by too vigorous growth.	Too severe pruning and/or excessive feeding.	Prune no more than absolutely necessary. Do not feed unless essential, and limit the amount of fertilizer to that recommended.
Failure to produce berries.	Lack of pollination, weather conditions or poor growing conditions.	Ensure that the shrub has the necessary neighbour(s) for cross-pollination. Protect from frost and ensure that the shrub does not suffer from drought. Check too that the soil and aspect are suitable.
Shoots dying back from the tips.	Frost and freezing wind	Cut away the dead shoots and protect the shrub with hessian or polythene.
Leaves or main shoots wilting.	Drought.	Water thoroughly and put down a thick mulch. Check that the container is large enough for tub shrubs.
Leaves small, yellowed and falling early.	Waterlogged soil.	Move the shrub to a drier position. Improve the soil surface by hoeing. Reduce the watering of shrubs in tubs.

Roses

The rose is without doubt the most popular shrub for planting in gardens. And no wonder. What other shrub or plant can provide a continuous display of colour for up to six months of the year? Moreover, roses will grow on most soils. The rose has been held in esteem and cultivated since the early days of gardening.

The roses in cultivation originated from wild roses, or what the nurseryman calls species roses. Species roses today also include those hybrids which have been produced by crossing one species with another. The colourful *Rosa rubrifolia* is a fine example of a true species rose. 'Old roses' were the results of the first attempts to produce a bedding or proper rose for the garden. They arose occasionally from natural mutations of wild roses, but more often from selective breeding.

From these old roses the hybrid tea roses were produced. Tea roses get their name from the fact that when they were first introduced, the scent reminded people of newly opened tea chests. These particular roses are still the best choice for perfume and quality of flowers. Floribunda roses were produced by crossing hybrid tea roses with the dwarf polyanthas. As the name floribunda implies, you get a cluster of flowers produced on each stem. If it is mainly colour you are after, these are by far the best choice. Floribundas generally cannot equal the hybrid tea roses for scent, but the more modern varieties have shapely blooms which are almost a match for the finest of the tea roses.

Modern shrub roses are generally hybrids between the species roses and the old roses. Most are repeat flowering and are in bloom from the beginning of summer until early autumn. Climbing and rambling roses are the ones that are at home against walls and fences. Some are descendents of climbing species. The vast majority, however, have been produced from hybrid teas and floribundas. Some are capable of growing to more than 9 m (30 ft), while some of the modern recurrent-flowering climbers rarely exceed 3 m (10 ft). Standard roses have erect, bare stems on top of which a particular rose variety has been budded, normally a hybrid tea or floribunda. However, to produce a weeping head, some standard roses are budded with a rambler variety. Standards have 90 cm to 1.2 m (3 to 4 ft) stems; half-standards have 75 to 85 cm (2½ ft to 2 ft 9 in) stems; weeping standards have 1.5 to 1.65 m (5 to 5½ ft) stems.

The best time for planting roses is in the late autumn and early spring during mild weather when the soil is workable. Roses bought in containers from garden centres can be planted at any time. The site for roses should be as open and sunny as possible, since roses need plenty of light and air if

Some recommended hybrid tea roses

Name	Attraction	Height
Alec's Red	cherry red, fragrant	medium
Alexander	vermilion	tall
Blessings	pink, fragrant	medium
Diorama	apricot, fragrant	medium
Ena Harkness	scarlet, fragrant	medium
Ernest H. Morse	red, fragrant	tall
Fragrant Cloud	orange red, fragrant	medium
Mischief	salmon, fragrant	medium
Mullard Jubilee	pink, fragrant	medium
Pascali	white	tall
Perfecta	cream, fragrant	tall
Whisky Mac	gold, fragrant	medium

Some recommended floribundas

Name	Attraction	Height
Allgold	yellow	low
Anne Crocker	red	tall
Arthur Bell	yellow, fragrant	tall
Dearest	salmon, fragrant	medium
Elizabeth of Glamis	salmon, fragrant	medium
Evelyn Fison	orange scarlet	medium
Iceberg	white	tall
Lilli Marlene	scarlet	medium
Orange Sensation	orange, fragrant	medium
Queen Elizabeth	pink	very tall
Tip Top	salmon, fragrant	low
Topsi	orange scarlet	low

Right: A climbing rose.

they are to be sturdy and avoid disease. The exception is near the coast, where roses may have to be planted in the shelter of a wall, fence or hedge as a protection from salt-laden winds.

If you have taken over an old garden which has rose beds which you wish to renovate, it is advisable to change as much of the soil as possible in the beds before planting, to avoid rose sickness. No one yet fully understands why, but roses grown where roses have been growing before simply fail

Some recommended climbers: Name / Attraction

Compassion, hybrid tea type blooms of apricot/salmon, fragrant, disease resistant foliage.

Danse de Feu, orange scarlet, very vigorous, good for a north facing wall.

Galway Bay, salmon pink, healthy foliage, good for a confined space.

Golden Showers, brilliant yellow flowers borne continuously, fragrant, compact and good for a small area of wall.

Handel, ivory blooms edged with carmine, bronze tinted foliage.

New Dawn, pink, very fragrant, moderate growth, free flowering.

Pink Perpetue, pink, fragrant, very vigorous, suitable for a north facing wall.

Schoolgirl, apricot, fragrant, vigorous growth.

Swan Lake, beautifully shaped white flowers flushed initially with pink, vigorous, constantly in bloom.

to flourish. One remedy is to remove some of the old soil and to replace it with plenty of rotted turf. This can be produced either in your own garden during the renovating work or by purchasing some cheap meadow turf which can be stacked, grass side to grass side, and rotted down. Rotted turf often gives better results with roses than compost or farm manure. In any case the beds for roses should be prepared well in advance by digging and, if necessary, by double digging where the drainage is poor. On heavy clay soils—contrary to popular opinion, not necessarily the best for roses—

improvements to the texture can be made by working in compost, peat or, best of all, strawy stable manure. Similarly, sandy soils should have plenty of organic material dug in to improve their ability to retain moisture.

If roses arrive from the nursery when the weather is unsuitable for planting, unpack them in a shed or garage, but keep the roots covered with damp sacking or straw. Should your soil be waterlogged, you can plant the roses, still bundled together, in the vegetable plot for a couple of weeks or so until conditions improve. Roses which have been stored

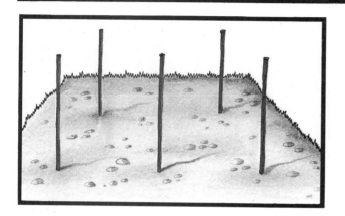

(1) **Before planting roses in a rose bed, mark out their approximate positions with sticks so that you get the spacing right. (See page 57 for spacing distances.) If you have three rows in a bed, stagger the middle row so that it does not line up with the other two. Also, try to keep roses of the same height together, or alternatively plant the shorter roses at the front of the bed.**

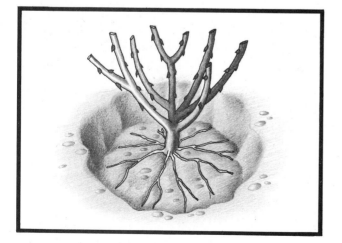

(2) **When planting, make a hole sufficiently large to take the roots of the rose easily once they are spread out. Put the soil from the hole**

into a barrow (rather than dump it on the bed which tends to upset the entire level of the bed). Check the roots of the rose for damage and trim with secateurs as necessary. Then place the rose in the hole so that the bud union or budding point with the rootstock is at soil level, or 3 cm (1 in) below soil level if your soil is light or sandy. Standard roses will need supporting with a sturdy stake (see illustrations 5 and 7, pages 31-2).

(3) **Fill in around the roots of the rose with a misture of soil and plenty of moist peat. A bucket of peat allotted to each rose may seem extravagant, but will guarantee you the best roses in the neighbourhood. As you fill in around the rose, give it a gentle shake occasionally to make sure there are no air pockets and that it is settled firmly. Tread the soil around the newly planted rose bush in a circle with your heel. However, take care not to upset its level in relation to the surrounding soil.**

indoors should have their roots soaked overnight in a bucket of water before planting.

Bush roses should be 38 to 45 cm (15 to 18 in) apart, depending on their eventual height. Standard roses should be 90 cm to 1.8 m (3 to 6 ft) apart. Old-fashioned and shrub roses should be around 1.2 m (4 ft) apart while climbers and ramblers need a separation of at least 1.8 m (6 ft).

Bush and standard roses need pruning every year. Old-fashioned and shrub roses need hardly any pruning at all apart from the occasional thinning out and the removal of dead wood.

Climbing roses too should not be pruned any more than is necessary, but merely thinned out and confined to their allotted space. A step-by-step guide to pruning roses and other shrubs is given in the next chapter.

Roses should be fed with a proprietary granular rose fertilizer in mid-spring and midsummer, or as directed by the manufacturers. Routine spraying with a systemic fungicide between mid-spring and early autumn will give protection to those roses susceptible to mildew and blackspot. Aphids and the numerous other insects which feast off roses

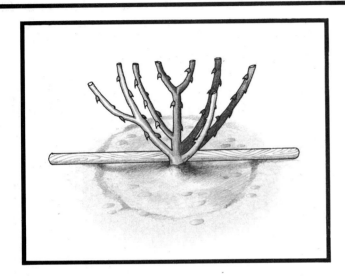

(4) Using a stick, check again that the union of the newly planted rose is level with the soil, or 3 cm (1 in) below if your soil is light or sandy. Then make an accurate measure from the centre of the bush to the point where you will plant the next bush.

there will seldom be occasion to remove suckers which spring from the wild rootstock on which the rose variety is grafted. If suckers appear (distinguishable by their leaves, colour, and often prickly stems, but most tellingly by their origin below the bud union), soil has to be scraped away gently from the base of the rose before the suckers can be pulled off. This is very important. If the suckers are cut off, they will simply reappear in greater numbers.

(5) If your bushes are planted at the correct depth and if you use mulches and refrain from forking or digging in your rose beds,

(6) An individual dose of proprietary rose fertilizer should be scattered around each rose bush in mid-spring just before you apply the annual mulch. A second application of granular fertilizer can be given in mid-summer just as the second flush of flowers is forming. Also in mid-spring, when the soil is moist, put down a mulch of moist moss peat

are best dealt with by spraying with a suitable insecticide, when they are first noticed. In mid-spring you can also treat the soil with a rose-bed weedkiller before putting down a 5 cm (2 in) thick moisture-giving and weed-suppressing layer of moist peat or garden compost around the bushes.

Bush roses are available in several heights from 38 cm to 1.2 m (15 in to 4 ft) tall. For convenience we can classify them as tall, medium or low growing.

Apart from the various bush and climbing roses, there are many beautiful roses which are largely ignored by the majority of gardeners. These are the shrub roses, many of which are the ancestors of our modern garden roses. They are called shrub roses because, unlike the modern bedding roses, they are most at home in the shrub border. These roses have a beauty of leaf and general outline which their modern cousins cannot equal. Some, such as the rugosas, also bear huge crops of rose hips which last well into winter, but, best of all, shrub roses are among the most deliciously fragrant of shrubs in the entire garden. Some are a mere 90 cm (3 ft) tall; others soar to a lofty 2.4 m (8 ft). You can mingle them with shrubs or give them a small circular bed all to themselves on the lawn.

---

around the roses 5 cm (2 in) thick to cut out the need for watering and to keep down weeds. The mulch may also fill in holes created by a rose bush rocking in the wind in wet soil.

(7) Routine spraying with a systemic fungicide should begin in spring and continue until early autumn to give the roses protection against black spot, mildew and rust which disfigure the leaves and rob the rose of some of its beauty. An insecticide can also be incorporated in the spray to give full protection too against all manner of pests. However, do try to spray in the evening.

(8) Remove (deadhead) the faded flowers of bush and climbing roses as soon as the petals start to fall, both for the general appearance of the garden and to encourage the production of more flowers. Cut just above a leaf and outward-facing bud. For established flori-bundas, remove the whole truss (flower clusters), but for hybrid tea roses, cut the shoots with the faded blooms to about half their length. Do not deadhead shrub roses.

Above: Rosa rugosa 'Sarah van Fleet'.

Recommended shrub roses		
Name	**Size**	**Attraction**
Rosa alba **'Maiden's Blush'**	1.5 m by 1.2 m (5 ft by 4 ft)	sweetly scented blush pink flowers in early and midsummer followed by red hips.
Rosa × *borboniana* **'Kathleen Harrop'**	1.8 m by 1.5 m (6 ft by 5 ft)	superbly scented flowers from early summer to late autumn; thornless.
Rosa california **'Plena'**	1.8 m by 1.8 m (6 ft by 6 ft)	deep rich pink fragrant flowers in early and midsummer followed by red hips.
Rosa centifolia **'Chapeau de Napoleon' (cabbage rose)**	1.8 m by 1.5 m (6 ft by 5 ft)	richly fragrant flowers in early and midsummer.
Rosa chinesis **'Cécile Brunner' (China or monthly rose)**	1.2 m by 1.2 m (4 ft by 4 ft)	scentless pink flowers; popularly called the Sweetheart Rose.
Rosa **'Constance Spry' (modern shrub rose)**	1.8 m by 1.2 m (6 ft by 4 ft)	pink fragrant flowers in early and midsummer.

Recommended shrub roses (continued)		
Name	Size	Attraction
Rosa damascena 'Madame Hardy' (Damask rose)	1.5 m by 1.2 m (5 ft by 4 ft)	richly scented white flowers in early and midsummer.
Rosa 'Fountain' (modern shrub rose)	1.5 m by 1.2 m (5 ft by 4 ft)	fragrant velvety blood red flowers from early summer to late autumn.
Rosa gallica 'Tuscany Superb' (Gallica or French rose)	1.2 m by 90 cm (4 ft by 3 ft)	richly scented velvety crimson purple flowers in early and midsummer.
Rosa 'Nevada' (modern shrub rose)	2.4 m by 1.2 m (8 ft by 4 ft)	masses of creamy white, faintly scented flowers in late spring and early summer and again in late summer.
Rosa rubiginosa (Sweet Briar or Eglantine rose)	2.4 m by 1.8 m (8 ft by 6 ft)	pink fragrant flowers in early summer followed by orange-scarlet hips; the foliage is aromatic.
Rosa rubrifolia	2.1 m by 1.5 m (7 ft by 5 ft)	scentless pink flowers in early summer followed by red hips; the stems of the rose are reddish violet and almost thornless, while the leaves are glaucous purple if the rose is grown in a sunny postion.
Rosa rugosa 'Frau Dagmar Hastrup' (Japanese or rugosa rose)	1.4 m by 1.4 m (4 ft by 4 ft)	fragrant rose pink flowers from early summer to mid-autumn followed by a huge crop of tomato-like red hips.
Rosa rugosa 'Roseraie de l'Hay'	1.8 m by 1.5 m (6 ft by 5 ft)	very fragrant crimson purple velvety blooms.
Rosa sericea pteracantha	2.4 m by 1.2 m (8 ft by 4 ft)	scentless creamy white flowers in late spring leading to black hips; the large, translucent ruby red thorns on the stems are most attractive in winter.
Rosa spinosissima 'Stanwell Perpetual'	1.2 m by 1.2 m (4 ft by 4 ft)	richly perfumed flowers from late spring to midsummer.
Rosa xanthina 'Canary Bird'	2.4 m by 1.8 m (8 ft by 6 ft)	superb show of brilliant yellow, scentless flowers in late spring and early summer.

Pruning Shrubs & Roses

If there is one problem which besets gardeners more than most, it is simply this: whether or not (as well as when and how) to prune shrubs. Pruning is the art of regulating plant growth to promote the desired result—be it to maintain plant health, or to train the plant, or to improve the quality of flowers, foliage or stems.

Surprisingly perhaps, the majority of shrubs do not need much pruning at all. Few of the evergreens do, except where a particular shrub has become overgrown. Then it is just a case of giving it a quick trim after flowering. Many of the slower growing deciduous shrubs also need little pruning: for example, azaleas, daphne, hibiscus, most hydrangeas, lilacs, magnolias, viburnums and witch hazels.

The shrubs and climbers which do need pruning are the fast unruly growers. These can be placed in separate groups for pruning purposes: *group one,* those which flower in spring and summer on shoots which were produced the previous year; and *group two,* those which flower after midsummer and in autumn on shoots grown during the current year.

Group one: Typical examples are *Clematis montana,* flowering currant, deutzia, jasmine, weigela and wisteria.

These can all be pruned immediately after flowering by cutting away all those shoots which have just flowered. Such shoots can be recognized because they are usually a darker colour than the new ones.

Group two: Typical examples are *Buddleia davidii,* deciduous ceanothus, fuchsia, lavender, *Lippia, Passiflora* (passion flower), perovskia and *Tamarix pentandra.*

The aim with these particular shrubs is to encourage them to make plenty of young shoots which in turn will bear most of the flowers. Pruning is normally carried out immediately before growth starts in spring.

Before you start to do any pruning, you need the right tools for the job. Really sharp secateurs are best for removing shoots and slender stems, while long-handled loppers are a wise investment for dealing with prickly shrubs such as roses and for getting at the centre of shrubs. A pruning saw will be necessary if you have to remove large branches.

When shortening a branch, cut just above an outward-facing bud or shoot. The cut itself should be made so that it is diagonally parallel with the bud or shoot.

Here then is a simplified six-stage guide to pruning with examples of shrubs which can be so treated.

Previous page: Pruning at the correct angle.

CATEGORY ONE: REMOVING DEAD, WEAK AND STRAGGLING GROWTH AND SHOOTS AFTER FLOWERING

Examples of shrubs which can be pruned by this method:

Abelia	*Garrya* (Californian catkin
Akebia	bush)
Amelanchier (Shadbush, June	*Hebe* (Veronica)
berry, Snowy mespilus)	*Hibiscus* (Tree hollyhock/
Arbutus (Strawberry tree)	Rose Mallow)
Buxus (Box)	*Hippophae* (Sea Buckthorn)
Callicarpa	*Ilex* (Holly)
Calluna	*Mahonia*
Ceanothus — evergreen	*Olearia* (Daisy bush)
Chaenomeles (Flowering	*Pyracantha* (Firethorn)
Quince, Japonica)	*Ribes* (Flowering currant)
Chimonanthus (Winter sweet)	*Rosmarinus* (Rosemary)
Choisya (Mexican orange)	*Salix* (Willow)
Clerodendron	*Sambucus* (Elder)
Cotinus (Smoke bush)	*Spartium* (Spanish broom)
Cotoneaster	*Symphoricarpus* (Snowberry)
Daphne	*Syringa* (Lilac)
Elaeagnus	*Tamarix tetranda* (Tamarisk)
Escallonia	*Viburnum*
Euonymus (Spindle-tree)	*Yucca* (Candles of the Lord)

This kind of pruning can be applied to the majority of shrubs, and may simply involve tidying or removing damaged branches.

(1) Make a routine examination in spring. Cut away any diseased, dead or damaged wood, cutting back to a healthy, outward-facing bud or shoot. Weak growth is best cut back to a main stem. Where branches have become straggly or unsightly, you can cut them back by as much as half their length to a strong, outward-facing bud or shoot.

CATEGORY TWO: RESTRICTING THE SIZE OF CLIMBERS

Examples of climbers which can be pruned by this method:

Actinidia

Aristolochia (Birthwort)

Campsis (Trumpet creeper)

Celastrus (Staff vine or climbing bittersweet)

Hedera (Ivy)

Hydrangea petiolaris

Jasminum (Jasmine)

Lonicera (Honeysuckle)

Parthenocissus (Virginian creeper)

Wisteria

Most climbers do not need any pruning until they become too large for their allotted space. Then you can prune immediately after flowering, or, in the case of non-flowering climbers, in spring or summer. Self-clinging climbers, such as Virginia creeper, climbing hydrangea and ivy should be trimmed on the wall in almost the same way as if you were cutting a hedge.

(2) Climbers, or for that matter wall shrubs, which need supports are best removed from their wires or trellis. Then all the side growths can be cut away to leave only the main stems. If these main branches are thick and old (in the case of a climber in an established garden) cut away some of them and retain some of the younger new shoots, growing either from soil level or from low down on the old stems. The pruned climber is then tied back on to the wall with its stems evenly spaced out.

CATEGORY THREE: PRUNING SHRUBS WHICH FLOWER ON NEW SHOOTS

Examples of shrubs which can be pruned by this method:

Buddleia davidii (Butterfly Bush)

Caryopteris

Ceanothus —deciduous

Ceratostigma (Hardy plumbago)

Colutea (Bladder Senna)

Cornus (Dogwood)

Fuchsia

Hydrangea paniculata

Lavandula (Lavender)

Lippia (Lemon-scented verbena)

Passiflora (Passion Flower)

Perovskia

Ruta (Rue)

Santolina (Lavender Cotton)

Senecio (Groundsel; ragwort)

Spiraea x bumalda

Tamarix pentandra (Tamarisk)

These particular shrubs flower on the new shoots which grow during the current season. For this reason, such shrubs are best pruned in spring, just as growth is beginning, to remove dead or frosted wood, to restrict their size and encourage better flowers.

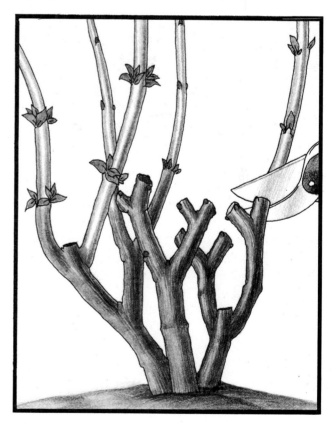

(3) With either secateurs or lopping shears, cut back all the previous year's shoots or branches to two or three buds from their base. With some shrubs, notably the caryopteris, fuchsia and perovskia, this may mean reducing them practically to ground level.

CATEGORY FOUR: PRUNING TO ENCOURAGE FLOWERS AND TO RESTRICT GROWTH

> **Examples of shrubs which can be pruned by this method:**
>
> *Clematis* (Virgin's Bower) hybrids
> *Cytisus* (Broom)
> *Deutzia*
> *Forsythia* (Golden Bells)
>
> *Jasminum* (Jasmine)
> *Kerria* (Jew's Mallow; bachelor's buttons)
> *Weigela*
> *Wisteria*

This type of pruning is an extension of the first category and may be termed the perfectionist's pruning group. For none of the shrubs actually needs pruning. The sole reason for pruning is to keep the shrubs tidy and to improve the quality of the flowers.

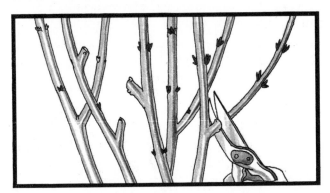

(4) The shrubs in this category flower on shoots produced during the previous year. So they can be most conveniently pruned immediately they finish flowering. The aim is to cut each shoot back to two or three buds from the point where it meets the parent branch.

CATEGORY FIVE: THINNING AND RENOVATING OVERGROWN SHRUBS

> **Examples of shrubs which can be thinned:**
>
> *Berberis* (Barberry)
> *Clethra* (White Alder; Sweet pepper)
> *Corylopsis*
> *Forsythia* (Golden Bells)
>
> *Genista* (Broom)
> *Hydrangea macrophylla*
> *Philadelphus* (Mock orange)
> *Ribes* (Flowering currant)
> *Rubus* (Blackberry)
>
> **Examples of shrubs which can be renovated:**
>
> *Arbutus* (Strawberry tree)
> *Aucuba*
> *Cornus* (Dogwood)
> *Lavandula* (Lavender)
>
> *Pernettya* (Prickly Heath)
> *Pieris*
> *Syringa* (Lilac)
> *Viburnum*

Some shrubs can become overgrown unless some of the oldest wood is occasionally thinned at ground level. With shrubs such as the forsythia and ribes, for instance, this may be a once-in-five-years' job, while with the hydrangea you may want to do it more often to restrict its size and improve the quality of the flowers. Renovating is a drastic form of pruning used mainly on evergreens which have either become straggly or have overgrown their allotted space.

(5) In spring cut out the selected mature branches which, on a hydrangea, can be identified by their coarser appearance and by the fact that they have both laterals (side-shoots) and sub-laterals (secondary side-shoots). Make your cuts within 3 cm (1 in) of the ground using either lopping shears or a pruning saw. On especially overgrown shrubs, younger branches can also be cut out from the centre.

Renovate evergreens in spring begin by cutting away all the top growth with lopping shears. Then, using a pruning saw, cut the branches down to within a few centimetres (inches) of the ground and paint the stumps with a special bituminous wound-sealing paint. It may be two or three years before shrubs which undergo this form of major surgery flower again.

Deciduous flowering and berrying shrubs can also be given this 'category five' treatment. However, they are best dealt with in the dormant period of mid- and late winter, and the cutting-back need not be quite so drastic.

CATEGORY SIX: PRUNING ROSES

When to prune: The best time to prune roses in mild districts is in late winter. However, in cold areas, it is better to wait until mid-spring. In fact it is impossible to make hard and fast rules about rose pruning as it is largely dependent on whether or not you get an early spring. The exceptions to the spring pruning routine are climbers, ramblers and weeping standards. Climbers are pruned lightly after they finish flowering and again in late winter or early spring.

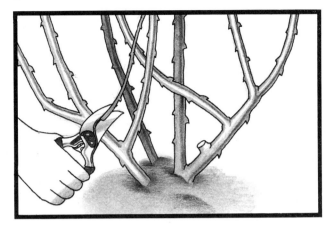

(6) How to prune correctly: Secateurs can be used for pruning slender shoots, but for the tougher wood use lopping shears. Make your cuts above the growth buds (found at the junction of a leaf with a stem) so that the cut is diagonally parallel with the bud. The buds should face outwards to encourage growth to spread away from the centre. The cut should be no more than 5 mm ($\frac{1}{4}$ in) above the bud; otherwise the shoot may die back. If you have to remove an entire branch, cut it back as close to the parent stem as possible and smooth the cut with a very sharp knife.

However, before you do any pruning at all, take a careful look at the bush or standard and decide what you are attempting to do. Prune all bushes and standards in the following three steps before treating each rose according to its type.

(7) Cut back any dead, damaged or diseased stems to a suitable healthy bud, or down to ground level if necessary.

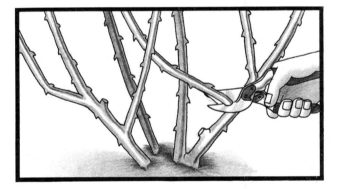

(8) Then cut out thin or weak stems to allow the rose to concentrate its energies on the more vigorous flower-producing branches. Prune to where they join a strong stem or the rootstock.

(9) Finally, cut away all those stems which cross into the centre of the bush or which rub against stronger stems. This prevention of overcrowding also helps to avoid disease.

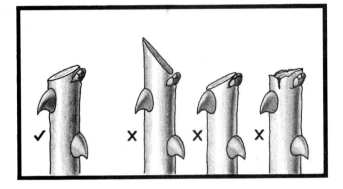

(10) How much to prune: Newly planted hybrid tea roses are pruned to about 10 cm (4 in) from the ground in spring. In future years, established hybrid tea roses, as a general guide, are cut back by about one-third of their growth annually. You will have

to use some common sense, for weak growth is cut back much harder than the more vigorous stems. The same rules apply to the hybrid tea standard roses.

Newly planted floribunda roses should be cut back to about 15 cm (6 in) from their base in spring. In future years, it is sufficient to prune them back by a quarter of their growth. The same goes for the established floribunda standard roses.

(11) The pruning of climbing roses should be a continual process. Newly planted climbers need no pruning during the first year, but in future late summers and autumns, trim back the shoots which have finished flowering to a suitable bud. In early winter, remove all dead and damaged wood. Then cut back the longest branches to a new shoot by as much as is necessary to restrict the rose to a given space. Side-shoots which have borne flowers should be cut back by about half their length.

(12) The pruning of rambler roses has one basic aim: to remove old wood in proportion to the new branches which have been formed. Newly planted ramblers need no pruning during their first year, but early in future autumns the work should be tackled accord-

66

ing to the growth and type of rose. For example, if the new growth comes direct from the base, cut the old branches which have borne flowers right down to the ground. If, on the other hand, new stems are produced from a point halfway up or lower on the old branches, cut back the old branches to that point. If a rambler produces little new growth at or near ground level, retain the strongest of the old branches and prune the side-shoots to two buds from the point where they meet the main stems.

(13) Delay the pruning of species and modern shrub roses as long as possible, as part of their attraction is their informal appearance. Many of these particular roses do not flower well on new wood and most of the blooms are produced on the previous year's side-shoots and later sub-laterals. The time for pruning, when it does become necessary, is between leaf-fall and early spring. It may be necessary to prune taller shrub roses in late autumn to reduce the bushes' wind resistance to winter storms.

First of all, remove all diseased and damaged wood. If an exceptionally long stem has been produced, prune it back by a third of its length to keep the shrub within bounds. Then, cut all the side-shoots which have borne flowers to a strong bud about 8 cm (3 in) from their parent branches. Lastly, cut a few centimetres off the tops of remaining stems to encourage them to produce side-shoots which will bear flowers the following year. With those shrub roses which bear attractive hips in autumn, pruning can be delayed until late winter so that you can get the full benefit of this very welcome display.

Flowers

For many people, growing flowers is real gardening: the chance to produce something of beauty from a tiny packet of seeds. These days you can raise most plants from seed, and a glance at a nursery catalogue will reveal what a simply superb choice you have.

The quickest way to convert any patch of bare soil into a riot of colour is to plant annuals. These are plants, as the name suggests, which complete their life cycle in one growing season. Annuals are usually sown outdoors, wherever they are to flower, in spring, and no other plant can equal them for the sheer number of flowers which they produce.

Annuals sown outdoors are classified as 'hardy'. Others which need some warmth to help germinate the seed are referred to as 'half-hardy'. You do not

need a heated greenhouse to raise half-hardy annuals. Most of them can be started very satisfactorily on a sunny windowsill indoors. Ideally you should have a cold frame, or a couple of large cloches, to harden off the plants in late spring before planting them in the garden in late spring or early summer when all risk of frost has passed.

Half-hardy annuals provide some of the most dazzling colours and most beautiful flowers in the garden. They are splendid for filling in the odd bare patch between shrubs, or for putting in window boxes, tubs and hanging baskets.

Biennials are like annuals in that they generally flower once and then die. However, unlike annuals, they normally take two years to flower. Biennials are best sown outdoors, in a small bed specifically set aside as a seed bed, in early or midsummer and transplanted to their final quarters in the autumn.

Biennials are especially useful in the garden because they often flower early in the year. Most can be sown in a small seed bed in a partially shaded position. Some such as the primrose are better started off in potting mixture indoors as if they were half-hardy annuals, and then transplanted to a small nursery bed, before being moved to their final position in the autumn.

Annuals and biennials do a magnificent job in filling the gaps in the garden and are ideal for a splash of colour in spring and summer. However, we also need perennials to produce a permanent background of colour, mainly in the late spring and autumn. The soil for perennial plants, or herbaceous plants as they are also called, must be well prepared as the plants generally remain undisturbed for a number of years.

Before perennials are set in place in early spring, break the soil down well with a fork. The plants themselves can be planted with a trowel. In mid-spring, give the plants a top dressing of granular general fertilizer at the rate of 135 gm per sq m (4 oz per sq yd) and surround them with a moisture-retaining and weed-suppressing layer of compost or moist peat.

Some perennial plants are unable to support the weight of their stems and will become an untidy tangle if left to their own devices. The most attractive way of staking perennial plants is to surround them with twiggy branches. Failing this, you can use bamboo canes, or wooden stakes and twine.

There are hundreds of different plants available from which you can make your choice. Here then is a number of selections for an assortment of different situations.

Left: Pelargonium, lobelia, tagetes and fuchsia in containers surround a doorway. Previous page: A wall of natural colour.

69

HARDY ANNUALS

NAME	HEIGHT AND SPREAD	COLOUR OF FLOWERS
Alyssum	10 cm by 30 cm (4 in by 12 in)	white, pink or lilac
Calendula (English or Pot Marigold)	23–60 cm by 15–30 cm (9–24 in by 6–12 in)	orange, yellow, apricot and cream
Candytuft	23–45 cm by 15–45 cm (9–18 in by 6–18 in)	mixed, but mainly red and carmine
Clarkia	30–90 cm by 23–60 cm (1–3 ft by 9–24 in)	blue, red, pink and white
Eschscholzia (Californian Poppy)	15–38 cm by 15 cm (6–15 in by 6 in)	yellow, pink, red, orange and scarlet
Godetia	23–60 cm by 15–30 cm (9–24 in by 6–12 in)	red, pink, orange and white
Gypsophila	23–45 cm by 45 cm (9–18 in by 18 in)	white or pink

(1) Before sowing hardy annuals outdoors, fork over the soil in early spring to a depth of 23 cm (9 in) and work in some moist peat to make the soil friable. Then, about two weeks before sowing, scatter some general fertilizer over the soil at the rate of 68 gm per sq m (2 oz per sq yd) and rake this in, so that at the same time you are able to produce a fine bed of soil for the seed. If the particular annuals prefer poor soil, omit the fertilizer.

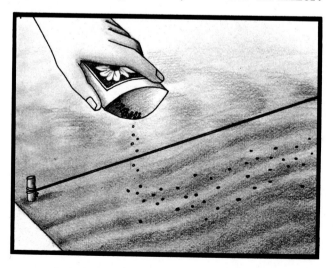

(2) Sow the seed of hardy annuals thinly, either in rows or by scattering the seed over the ground to produce a bold drift of colour.

WHEN TO SOW	POSITION	GROWING TIP
mid and late spring	full sun in ordinary soil	dead-head with scissors to make the plants bushy and to ensure continuous flowering
early and mid spring	sun or light shade in poor soil	remove the first flowers to make the plants bushy
early to late spring	full sun in poor soil	splendid choice for city gardens
early to late spring	full sun in ordinary soil	support tall plants with pieces of brushwood, or canes and twine; remove dead heads regularly with scissors
early to late spring	full sun in poor soil	let the plants self-seed as they will flower again in the autumn
early and mid-spring	full sun in light soil	allow the plants to self-seed to produce autumn flowers
early and mid-spring	full sun in ordinary soil	if the soil is 'acid', add a little lime before sowing

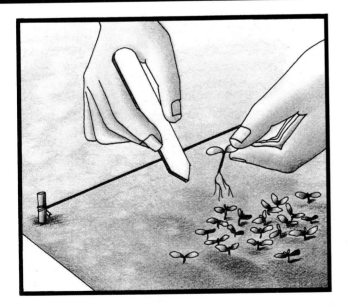

(3) When the seedlings have produced 'true' leaves, in addition to their oval seedling leaves, it is time to thin them out. The thinnings of some plants such as marigolds can be transplanted; discard others.

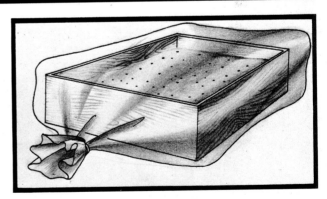

(4) With modern peat-based potting mixtures, the raising of half-hardy annuals could not be simpler. All you need is a seed tray, potting mixture and a packet of seeds. Fill the tray with mixture, firm it gently and water lightly if necessary to make it moist but not wet. Then sprinkle the seeds as thinly as possible over the potting mixture. Do not cover little seeds, the size of pepper grains, with mixture. Larger seeds may need to be covered to a depth of 5 mm ($\frac{1}{4}$ in). The

HARDY ANNUALS

NAME	HEIGHT AND SPREAD	COLOUR OF FLOWERS
Helichrysum ('everlasting' straw flower)	45–90 cm by 23–30 cm (1½–3 ft by 9–12 in)	pink, crimson, orange and white
Larkspur (annual delphinium)	23–90 cm by 30–38 cm (9–36 in by 12–15 in)	blue, red and white
Mignonette	30–38 cm by 15–23 cm (12–15 in by 6–9 in)	yellow, tinged with red, red and green
Nasturtium	15 cm to 2 m by 15–60 cm (6 in to 6 ft by 6–24 in)	yellow, pink, red, orange and various other shades
Nigella (love-in-a-mist)	23–45 cm by 23–30 cm (9–18 in by 9–12 in)	blue, pink, white, red, mauve and purple
Sunflower	60 cm to 3 m by 30–60 cm (2–10 ft by 1–2 ft)	yellow, primrose, bronze and maroon
Sweet Peas	60 cm to 2 m by 60–90 cm (2–6 ft by 2–3 ft)	white, cream, pink, red and lavender

next step is to cover the tray with a piece of polythene to retain moisture and to prevent the mixture from drying out. Since most half-hardy annuals require a temperature of around 18°C (64°F) to germinate the seed, the tray is best placed in a warm dark spot.

remove the polythene and move the tray and the seedlings to a warm, sunny windowsill. When the seedlings have produced 'true' leaves, it is time to transplant them to seed trays containing a peat-based potting mixture. Prepare the trays as for sowing seed.

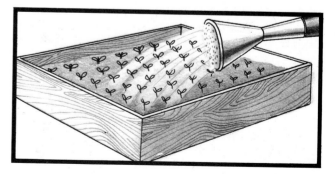

(5) Inspect the tray from time to time, and as soon as the first specks of life appear,

(6) Each little seedling should be 'pricked out' and planted gently about 5 cm (2 in) apart

WHEN TO SOW	POSITION	GROWING TIP
early to late spring	full sun in ordinary soil	cut the flowers before they are fully open; then dry, by hanging upside down, for winter decoration
early and mid-spring	full sun in ordinary soil	remove flowers as they fade to prolong the display
early and mid-spring	full sun in rich alkaline soil	if your soil is 'acid', add lime before sowing
mid and late spring	full sun in poor soil	use the climbing varieties to conceal ugly fences
early to late spring	full sun in ordinary soil	dead-head with scissors to ensure continuous bloom
mid-spring	full sun in rich, well-drained soil	place three seeds at each flowering position and thin out later to leave one plant
mid-spring	full sun in well-prepared, rich soil	remove faded blooms and do not allow the plants to produce seed pods; water thoroughly in dry spells

from its neighbours. Small seedlings, such as lobelia, can be pricked out in groups of three and four. For this job you can use either a pencil, the point of a seed row label, or the blade of a small screwdriver. It is important to hold the plants lightly by the leaf, not by their stems. You can afford to break a leaf; but break the main stem and you have lost the plant. After transplanting, the seedlings can be watered from a watering can fitted with a fine rose, and the seed tray placed on a windowledge out of direct sunlight for a day or two until the seedlings take firm root.

By late spring you can put the seed trays outside by day to acclimatize the plants to outdoor living, taking them indoors again at night. If you have a garden frame or cloches, the seed trays can be placed under

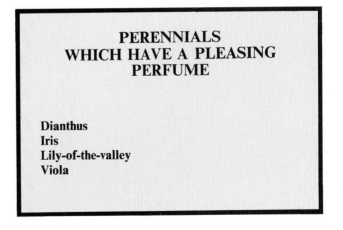

**PERENNIALS
WHICH HAVE A PLEASING
PERFUME**

Dianthus
Iris
Lily-of-the-valley
Viola

them for protection until the risk of frost has passed and the plants can be set out in their flowering positions in soil prepared in the same way as for sowing hardy annuals (see illustration 1).

HALF-HARDY ANNUALS

NAME	HEIGHT AND SPREAD	COLOUR OF FLOWERS
Antirrhinum (snapdragon)	15–60 cm by 23–30 cm (6–24 in by 9–12 in)	white, yellow, orange, red and mauve
Aster	23–60 cm by 30–45 cm (9–24 in by 12–18 in)	available in all colours
Dahlia	30–60 cm by 30–60 cm (1–2 ft by 1–2 ft)	yellow, pink, red, lilac, white and mixed shades
Lobelia	10–15 cm by 15–30 cm (4–6 in by 6–12 in)	shades of blue, red and white
Marigolds (French and African)	15–75 cm by 15–45 cm (6–30 in by 6–18 in)	many shades of yellow, orange and maroon
Mesembryanthemum (Livingstone Daisy)	7.5–10 cm by 25–30 cm (3–4 in by 9–12 in)	all colours and various shades
Nemesia	23–45 cm by 10–15 cm (9–18 in by 4–6 in)	blue, various bicolours and mixed
Petunia	15–30 cm by 30 cm (6–12 in by 12 in)	all colours and some bicolours
Phlox	15–30 cm by 23 cm (6–12 in by 9 in)	all colours in various shades
Salvia	23–45 cm by 23–45 cm (9–18 in by 9–18 in)	red, pink, scarlet, purple and lavender
Zinnia	23–75 cm by 15–30 cm (9–30 in by 6–12 in)	various, but mainly shades of yellow, red and orange

WHEN TO SOW	POSITION	GROWING TIP
late winter and early spring	sunny in ordinary soil	pinch out the centres of the plants to make them bushy
early and mid-spring	sunny, sheltered and in well-drained soil	remove the dead flowers early to prolong the floral display
early and mid-spring	sunny or light shade in soil enriched with plenty of compost	water freely in dry spells; lift the tubers in autumn after the first frosts and dust with green sulphur before storing in the garage, or shed, in boxes of dry peat for planting the following year
late winter and early spring	partial shade in rich soil	superb plants for window boxes and hanging baskets
early spring	sunny in well-drained soil	regular dead-heading encourages the plants to produce more flowers
late winter and early spring	full sun in hot dry soil	excellent plant for rockeries and the edge of paths
late winter to mid-spring	sunny in slightly acid soil	cut back the plants after flowering to promote fresh growth and more flowers
mid-winter to early spring	sheltered and sunny in ordinary soil	excellent for window boxes and hanging baskets; the plants are also among the best at surviving droughts
early and mid-spring	sunny in well-drained soil	feed with liquid fertilizer in summer to promote more flowers
mid-winter to early spring	sunny in ordinary soil	pinch off the tops of the plants when they are 7.5 cm (3 in) tall to make them bushy
early and mid-spring (outdoors late spring)	sunny and sheltered in rich soil	dead-heading encourages further flowers

BIENNIALS

some of the biennials which should give consistently good results and provide plenty of colour

NAME	HEIGHT AND SPREAD	COLOUR OF FLOWERS
Forget-me-not	15–30 cm by 15–23 cm (6–12 in by 6–9 in)	several shades of blue
Foxglove	90 cm to 1.5 m by 45 cm (3–5 ft by 18 in)	white, cream, pink, apricot, yellow, red and purple
Hollyhock	90 cm to 1.8 m by 30–45 cm (3–6 ft by 1–1½ ft)	white, yellow, scarlet, salmon, pink rose and deep red
Pansy	15–23 cm by 23–30 cm (6–9 in by 9–12 in)	most colours, single shades and blotched
Primrose (including polyanthus)	15–30 cm by 23 cm (6–12 in by 9 in)	all shades, both mixed and single
Sweet William	30–60 cm by 23 cm (1–2 ft by 9 in)	red, pink and white
Wallflower	23–60 cm by 23 cm (9–24 in by 9 in)	yellow, orange, red, russet and purple

PERENNIALS WHICH LIKE SUNSHINE

NAME	ATTRACTION
Achillea	yellow or white flowers
Aster	blue, pink, red or violet flowers
Chrysanthemum (the Shasta Daisies)	white flowers
Columbine	many rich colours
Delphinium	blue shades, white or pink flowers
Iris	flowers of all colours
Lupins	flowers of most colours
Sedum	red, pink, or yellow flowers

PERENNIALS WHICH THRIVE IN SHADE

NAME	ATTRACTION
Acanthus	mauve flowers
Anemone	pink or white flowers
Astilbe	red, pink or white flowers
Hellebore	pink, white, purple or maroon flowers
Lamium	inconspicuous flowers, but attractive silvery white leaves
Ornamental grasses (such as avena, carex, miscanthus)	foliage

WHEN TO SOW	POSITION	GROWING TIP
late spring to midsummer	partial shade in soil enriched with peat	plant together with tulips and wallflowers or around Mollis and Ghent azaleas for a dazzling display
late spring and early summer	light shade and moisture-retaining soil	put a layer of moist peat around the roots of the plants to stop them from wilting
late spring and early summer	sunny and sheltered in rich soil	dead-head to prevent self-seeding
early to midsummer	sun or partial shade in good soil	dead-head regularly to maintain flowering
indoors mid to late spring (slow to germinate); move to a shaded spot in midsummer	sun or partial shade in soil enriched with plenty of peat	water plants frequently in dry weather; protect flowers from birds with small sticks and black cotton
late spring and early summer	sunny in ordinary soil, containing preferably a little lime	remove all the flowers promptly as they fade
late spring and early summer	sunny in any well-drained soil	pinch off the growing points of the plants at 15 cm (6 in) to encourage side-shoots; acid soils are best given a top dressing of lime at the rate of 112 gm/m² (4 oz to a sq yd)

PERENNIALS WHICH NEED NO STAKING

NAME	ATTRACTION
Doronicum	yellow flowers
Day Lilies	flowers with several colour combinations
Erigeron	blue, violet or pink flowers
Euphorbia	green, yellow or orange flowers
Paeony	red, pink or white flowers
Salvia	blue, violet or pink flowers

PERENNIALS WHICH COVER THE SOIL AND ELIMINATE THE NEED FOR WEEDING

Brunnera
Geum
Geranium (herbaceous, NOT the houseplant)
Iberis
Nepeta
Pulmonaria

PERENNIALS WHICH GROW WELL IN DAMP POSITIONS

NAME	ATTRACTION
Astilbe	red, pink or white flowers
Gunnera	ornamental foliage resembling rhubarb
Hellebore	pink, white, purple or maroon flowers
Primula	scarlet, orange, violet, purple, mauve or yellow flowers, depending on the species
Sidalcea	crimson, salmon or pink flowers
Trollius	bright orange or deep yellow flowers

PERENNIALS WHICH HAVE BEAUTIFUL LEAVES

NAME	ATTRACTION
Acanthus	dark green, deeply divided leaves
Astilbe	fern-like leaves
Bergenia	red, purplish or bronze evergreen leaves
Hosta	leaves in bluish green, and combinations of green, cream, yellow and white
Lamium	white fleecy leaves
Paeony	green or bronze divided foliage
Ornamental grasses	leaves of blue, grey, silver, gold, purple and various stripes

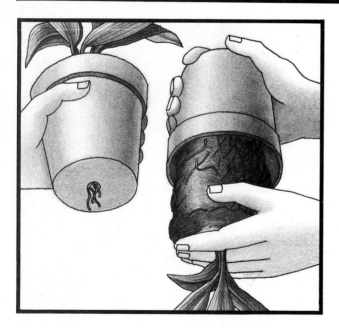

(7) Once a houseplant makes very little new growth and the compost dries out quickly and roots start to appear through the hole in the bottom of the pot, you know for certain that it needs to be repotted. Younger houseplants should be repotted annually in spring. Mature plants may need repotting every other year or so. First invert the pot, and holding the stem of the plant firmly between your fingers, shake out the soil and root ball.

(8) Gently ease away some of the old potting mixture from around the roots. Then place the plant on some mixture in a pot one size bigger and gradually add more mixture around the sides of the pot, firming the mixture with your fingers. Finally, water the pot thoroughly.

(9) Hanging baskets of living flowers make

78

Above: A bed of annuals in glorious display.

PERENNIALS WHICH ARE SUITABLE FOR ROCKERIES AND THE EDGE OF SHRUB AND FLOWER BEDS	
NAME	ATTRACTION
Alyssum	chrome yellow flowers
Aubretia	blue, mauve or violet flowers
Campanula	blue or mauve flowers
Iberis	white flowers
Saxifrage	yellow, red, pink or white flowers
Sedum	yellow or rosy red flowers
Thyme	crimson, lavender, mauve or white flowers

PERENNIALS WHICH HAVE THE BEST FLOWERS FOR CUTTING	
NAME	ATTRACTION
Aster	blue, violet, red or pink flowers
Coreopsis	yellow flowers
Dicentra	plum crimson, red or white flowers
Helenium	red or yellow flowers
Phlox	orange, scarlet, red, purple, lilac, pink or white flowers
Pyrethrum	red, salmon or pink flowers
Scabious	shades of blue or white flowers

an attractive addition to your home, whether suspended from a bracket on an outside wall or from a hook on the ceiling of the porch. The bowl-shaped baskets are made of galvanized wire and are sold by most hardware and garden shops. The first job is to line the basket with damp sphagnum moss, obtainable from flower shops or found growing wild. Next, place a piece of green polythene, slit with numerous drainage holes, against the moss, to prevent compost from being washed out of the basket when you add water. Pack the basket with moist peat-based potting mixture and firm it with your fingers.

(10) **Start to plant the basket around the edges with trailing plants such as lobelia, pendulous begonias or ivy-leaved and trailing pelargoniums (more commonly known as geraniums). Put a centre plant such as a dwarf fuchsia in the middle of the basket and surround it with such plants as petunias**

and begonias. Water the basket thoroughly. Since the plants which have been suggested here are frost-tender, the basket in this case cannot go outdoors until the end of spring or early summer. Water frequently in summer and feed with a liquid fertilizer.

(11) **Before planting in ornamental containers, whether large saucer-like bowls or conventional tubs, the first consideration is drainage. Place a layer of stones, gravel or broken flower pots at the foot of the container and then fill to about 3 cm (1 in) from the top with a suitable potting soil. Troughs and window boxes should be prepared for planting in the same way, except that in the case of window boxes use peat-based potting mixture because of the saving in weight. For maximum effect, plant the boxes with a mixture of dwarf and trailing plants, much as if you were planting a hanging basket.**

Bulbs

There are few greater pleasures in life than being able to admire the brilliant show put on by the spring flowering bulbs—snowdrops, crocuses, daffodils, hyacinths, irises and tulips are some of the most popular—all mingling happily among shrubs and other border plants.

Above: Kaufmanniana or Water-lily tulips.
Previous page: Storing gladioli bulbs.
Below right: Narcissus 'February Gold'.

The word 'bulb' is a general term which will be used here for all obviously bulb-like organs. As well as true bulbs (such as those of the tulip, hyacinth or narcissus) these include corms (such as those of the crocus and gladioli), rhizomes and tubers (the dahlia's, for instance) which are alike in being the forms that certain plants take when dormant. They are all abbreviated stems, packed with food reserves, ready for rapid growth when conditions are right. Bulbs must be stored in cool, dry conditions so they neither rot nor begin to sprout prematurely. Most are planted during their dormant period.

The smaller bulbs, such as the snowdrops, winter aconites, scillas, crocuses and rises, are best planted

in small groups in parts of the garden where they can be left undisturbed and allowed to multiply over the years. The dazzling colours of these bulbs can make the garden come suddenly alive and sparkle in every burst of sunshine. Yellow and cream daffodils and narcissus look best surrounded by the green of grass or with a dark background of conifers and hedges. Tulips can be planted in shrub or herbaceous beds and also in tubs on patios. Some of the so-called botanical tulips are a far better choice for small gardens than the tall Darwins, so vulnerable to blustery weather.

Tulipa praestans 'Fusilier', for instance, grows to a mere 15 cm (6 in) tall, yet it bears two to four orange-scarlet flowers on a single stem. Consider too some of the *T. greigii* and hybrid tulips. 'Perlina' at 25 cm (10 in) tall has heads of an eye-catching silvery salmon-rose colour and, as an added attraction, the leaves are blotched with chocolate brown.

The great advantage of these particular tulips is that unlike Cottage, Darwin, Lily, Parrot, Rembrandt or Triumph varieties, they do not need to be lifted after flowering. Instead they can be left safely in the ground to multiply.

When choosing daffodils and narcissus, do not overlook the smaller varieties of the *N. cyclamineus* species ('February Gold', 'Jenny', 'Little Witch' and 'Peeping Tom', for example) and also the scented jonquils. If selecting taller daffodils, it is worth paying a bit more to get some of the better and more attractive varieties.

Most spring-flowering bulbs should be planted in late summer and early autumn for best results the

---

BULBS CALENDAR GUIDE to which bulbs flower when

Mid-winter

Crocus ancyrensis
Snowdrops
Winter aconites

Late winter

Crocus biflorus
Crocus chrysanthus varieties
Crocus sieberi varieties
Iris reticulata hybrids
Narcissus cyclamineus varieties
Scillas
Tulipa (tulip) Violet Queen

Early spring

Anemone blanda varieties
Crocus tomasinianus varieties
Dutch crocus
Muscari (grape hyacinth)
Narcissus varieties (including daffodils)
Tulipa praestans varieties
Tulipa kaufmanniana (water-lily tulip) hybrids

Mid-spring

Anemone apennina
Anemone de Caen and St Brigid varieties
Erythronium dens-canis (dog's-tooth violet)
Fritillaria species
Hyacinths
Narcissus varieties (including jonquils)
Ornithogalum nutans (Star of Bethlehem)
Tulipa species
Tulipa fosteriana hybrids
Tulipa greigii hybrids
    also Early, Mendel, Triumph and Darwin tulips

Late spring

Allium
Narcissus varieties
Ornithogalum arabicum
Sparaxis
    also Darwin, Cottage, Rembrandt, Parrot and Lily-flowered tulips

Early summer

Gladiolus nanus varieties
Lilium (lily) varieties

Midsummer

Begonia
Chincherinchee
Gladioli (Butterfly, Large-flowered and Primulinus hybrids)
Lilium varieties
Montbretia (Crocosmia)

Late summer

Dahlia
Freesia (outdoor)
Lilium varieties

Autumn

Colchicum autumnale (Autumn crocus)
Nerine bowdenii
Schizostylis coccinea (kaffir lily)
Sternbergia lutea

following spring. Tulips are the exception. They give a better initial performance if you delay planting until late autumn.

When planting bulbs, many people tend to forget the summer-flowering ones. Yet flowers such as lilies are the most powerfully scented and beautiful of all the plants which are grown from bulbs. Most lily varieties should be planted in mid-autumn (the exception is the Madonna lily *Lilium candidum*, which should be planted in late summer), in soil lightened by the addition of peat. Place the bulbs in prepared holes so that they lie at a depth of three times the height of the bulb, which could be 15 cm (6 in) deep. Again Madonna lilies are the exception: they should be covered with just 5 cm (2 in) of soil. Once planted, lilies should not be disturbed. Feeding too is unnecessary. Simply give them a covering of 10 cm (4 in) of moist peat every spring.

Gladioli are another group of summer bulbs well

(1) If you want to have bulbs in flower indoors over winter or in early spring, plant them in bowls containing bulb fibre in early or mid-autumn. Crocuses, daffodils, hyacinths and tulips are the best bulbs for indoors. Many bulb suppliers also sell 'prepared' bulbs which have been advanced in their growth cycle so that they will flower indoors in winter. Fill the chosen container with moistened (but not wet) bulb fibre to 5 cm (2 in) to the top and stand the bulbs on the potting mixture so that they are almost touching. Then fill the space between and around the bulbs with more bulb fibre and wrap the container in several thicknesses of newspaper.

(2) The container should then be kept in a cool dark place, such as a garage, where the temperature is not more than 9°C (48°F), until the first shoots are well through the necks of the bulbs. If you cannot maintain such an initial low temperature, it is best to put the bulbs in their containers in a 'plunge bed' outdoors. This is made by digging a trench, one spit deep, placing bulb containers wrapped in newspaper in the bottom and filling in the trench with peat. 'Prepared' bulbs should remain in the dark of the plunge bed or garage for about 10 weeks. Ordinary bulbs should be kept covered for 15 weeks before bringing them into subdued light for a few days. Then move them to a well-lit position, where the temperature is around 18°C (64°F). Unfortunately most bulbs are not happy in the hot-house atmosphere of some centrally heated rooms.

worth planting from early to late spring 10 to 15 cm (4 to 6 in) deep in clumps or rows, and 20 cm (8 in) apart. The idea of planting over several months is to give a succession of flowers from midsummer to the first frosts, when the bulbs should be lifted.

Because the dahlia has tuberous roots which allow it to be lifted and stored from year to year, it too can be thought of as a bulb. The tubers should be started into growth in boxes of moist peat stood on a sunny window ledge in mid-spring. In late spring or early summer, when the risk of frost has passed, they can be planted outdoors 5 cm (2 in) deep in well-prepared rich soil with 30 to 60 cm (1 to 2 ft) between the plants, depending on their eventual height. Tall plants require sturdy stakes. Regular watering is vital to keep the plants growing strongly.

Another tuberous rooted plant is the begonia. The corms, or bulbs, should be pressed, hollow side

(3) When bulbs are to be planted in grassed areas, it is advisable to plant them in ragged drifts, not rigid rows or clumps. With daffodils, you can use a special bulb-planting tool (an open-ended cylinder which pulls up a 'plug' of soil which can be replaced on top of the implanted bulb) or trowel. With smaller bulbs, it is simpler to ease up a layer of the turf with a spade, loosen the soil with a fork, plant the bulbs, and firm down the turf. Remember that if bulbs are grown in lawns, the grass cannot be cut until all the bulb foliage has died back; otherwise the bulbs will be unable to replenish their food store and will not flower the following year.

(4) Some bulbous plants, such as the popular dahlia, will not survive winter frost. When the stems of dahlias are blackened by the first frosts, dig up the tubers, cut off most of the stems, and allow the tubers to dry sufficiently for you to brush off any remaining soil. Next dust the tubers with green sulphur as a precaution against fungal attack and store the tubers in a box of dry peat in a cool, frost-free place.

uppermost, into 7.5 cm (3 in) diameter peat pots, containing peat-based mixture, in mid-spring and started into growth in a light, frost-free place. The plants can be put outdoors in early summer, either in the open ground, or in tubs, window boxes and hanging baskets.

Bulbs growing in tubs provide a magnificent spring display. The tubs can be filled with either good garden soil or a suitable potting mixture, and the bulbs planted at the same depth as for those growing in ordinary beds and borders. It is for this reason that it is not a good idea to grow daffodils in window boxes. With shallow containers, it would be better to concentrate on growing some of the many smaller bulbs.

Where bulbs are grown in shrub and herbaceous borders and beds, the soil should be forked over first and improved if necessary by the addition of some peat, before planting the bulbs at the appropriate depths.

(5) After the first frosts, begonia corms should be lifted, dried and stored in a box of peat for planting the following year. Gladioli plants should be lifted when the foliage turns brown and allowed to dry out completely. Then cut off the dried tops 2.5 cm (1 in) above the corms and store the corms in paper bags in a dry, frost-free place for the following year.

Most other bulbs are best left in their original planting positions. If bulbs such as daffodils and tulips are in tubs which are required for summer plants, the bulbs can be lifted and planted in another part of the garden until their foliage dies down naturally. At this point the bulbs can be lifted again, dried and stored until the appropriate planting time comes around again.

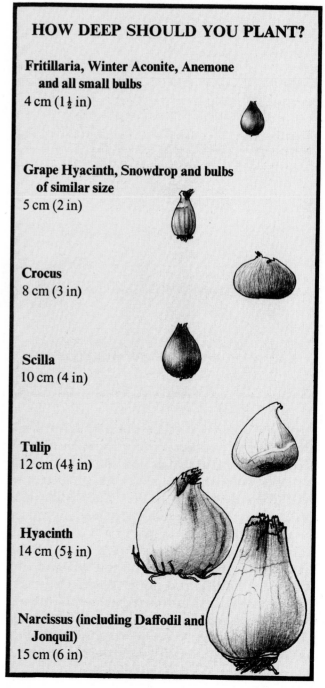

HOW DEEP SHOULD YOU PLANT?

Fritillaria, Winter Aconite, Anemone and all small bulbs
4 cm (1½ in)

Grape Hyacinth, Snowdrop and bulbs of similar size
5 cm (2 in)

Crocus
8 cm (3 in)

Scilla
10 cm (4 in)

Tulip
12 cm (4½ in)

Hyacinth
14 cm (5½ in)

Narcissus (including Daffodil and Jonquil)
15 cm (6 in)

Propagation

There are possibly a dozen different ways in which you can increase, virtually for free, the plants and shrubs which you already have in the garden, and you can also benefit from the cuttings obtained from friends' gardens. In this chapter we shall concern ourselves only with the easiest methods.

Above: Keeping cuttings warm. Previous page: Propagating perennials on a large scale.

Most plants and some shrubs readily propagate themselves. With cuttings, it is easier these days to get them to root, thanks to the development of rooting powders and liquids, which contain plant hormones. Once applied to the base of the cutting, the hormones encourage root formation. Your best plan is to buy a rooting agent which suits all cuttings, including those called 'softwood' and 'hardwood' cuttings. In any case the manufacturers normally list the plants and shrubs under the appropriate treatment.

Some plants and shrubs can be propagated outdoors; others need the warmth and shelter of indoors. Indoor propagation does create certain problems. For a start, some cuttings need plenty of light. So that means rooting them on a well-lit windowsill. However, you have to watch that the sun is not so bright that the cuttings become

HARDWOOD CUTTINGS
plants you can propagate by this method:

Buddleia
Cornus (Dogwood)
Deutzia
Forsythia
Lavandula (Lavender)
Ligustrum (Privet)
Lonicera (Honeysuckle)
Paeonia—the shrub
Philadelphus (Mock orange)
Polygonum
Potentilla
Ribes (Flowering currant)
Rosmarinus (Rosemary)
Sambucus (Elder)
Spiraea
Stephanandra
Tamarix (Tamarisk)
Weigela

HARDWOOD CUTTINGS

(1) Take your hardwood cuttings by selecting a hard and woody stem with buds all along its length and remove about 30 cm (12 in) of it with your secateurs.

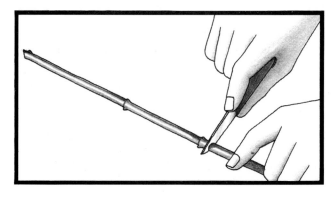

(2) Then trim the cutting, using a sharp knife, so that you sever it above a bud at the top end and below a bud at the base. Cuttings of evergreen shrubs should be cut above and below a leaf, and all the leaves should be removed from the lower half. If the shrub has particularly large leaves, such as those of the Portugal laurel, each leaf should be reduced in size by half with a sharp knife to minimize moisture loss while the cuttings are taking root.

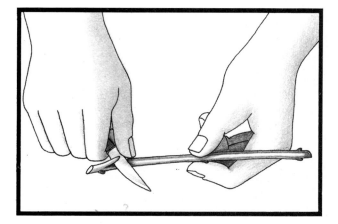

(3) If cuttings from certain plants prove difficult to root, you can make use of a technique called 'wounding'. All you have to do is to remove a thin sliver of bark near the base of the cutting. Finally the prepared cuttings, either 'wounded' or not, can be dipped in rooting agent.

scorched. There is a simple rule to remember, which may save you a lot of bother. If a mature plant or shrub grows in shade, the cuttings will thrive in shade. Similarly if a plant or shrub revels in full sun, the cuttings will usually prefer full sun.

When getting cuttings to root, or you are sowing seed, good hygiene is vital to prevent any possibility of disease. Use clean seed trays and pots, sterilized potting mixture when necessary and, if using a greenhouse or garden frame, maintain a well-ventilated atmosphere. Should grey mould be a problem, you can use an appropriate proprietary fungicide.

The takings of softwood cuttings offers a good

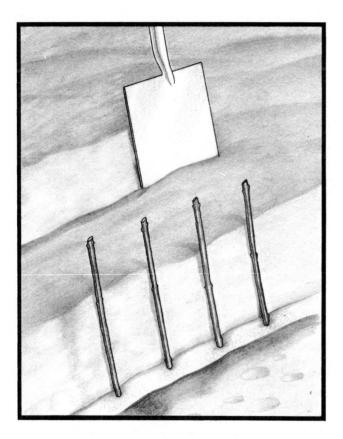

(5) In the autumn of the next year, those cuttings which by their new growth have obviously taken root can be lifted and planted elsewhere in the garden. The weaker looking cuttings are best left in the soil for a further year.

SOFTWOOD CUTTINGS

(4) The next step is to insert the cuttings in a previously prepared spot in the garden, ideally sheltered from cold winds. The 'cuttings bed' is prepared by pushing a spade at an angle to its full depth in the soil and then pushing it forwards slightly so that you are left with a V-shaped slip trench when you remove the spade. Next put a 5 cm (2 in) layer of sharp sand in the bottom and stand the cuttings about 7.5 cm (3 in) apart so that they are about two-thirds of their length below ground. Then fill the trench with soil and firm the area with your foot. Should winter frosts lift the soil in the proximity of the cuttings, you may have to firm it again carefully with your fingers to avoid damaging any roots. Keep cuttings free from weeds and make sure they are never short of water in dry spells.

(6) Take your softwood cuttings by selecting young, firm non-flowering shoots around 7.5 cm (3 in) long. Cut the shoot with four or five pairs of leaves with a sharp knife or secateurs.

90

SOFTWOOD CUTTINGS

plants you can propagate by this method:

Abelia
Anchusa
Ceanothus
Chrysanthemum
Dahlia
Delphinium
Euonymus
Fuchsia
Hypericum
Impatiens (Busy lizzie)
Lippia
Lupinus (Lupin)
Passiflora (Passion flower)
Pelargonium
Penstemon
Perovskia
Phygelius (Cape figwort)
Scabiosa (Scabious)
Solanum
Tradescantia species

way of propagating some herbaceous plants, shrubs such as the fuchsia and house or perennial summer bedding plants like the pelargonium. Such cuttings are normally taken in early summer.

Hardwood cuttings are, however, by far the easiest way of increasing most popular shrubs. The cuttings are normally taken in mid-autumn when

(9) The prepared cutting should then be potted in a 7.5 cm (3 in) diameter plastic pot containing moist peat-based cuttings compost and covered. Some plastic pots can be bought with clear plastic covers. Alternatively you can make a polythene tent by inserting two half-hoops of wire into the pot and covering with a clear polythene bag, secured to the pot with an elastic band.

(7) Slice the shoot diagonally just below the bottom pair of leaves and then pull off the lowest leaves, taking care not to tear the stem.

(8) Next dip the base of the cutting into either a liquid or powder hormone rooting agent.

(10) The pot should be kept in a well-lit position away from the scorching rays of the

91

the shrubs have stopped growing, although some shrubs will actually grow from cuttings taken at any time during the autumn or winter.

Unfortunately one comes across those difficult shrubs such as aucuba and choisya which will not root so readily from hardwood cuttings. The answer in such cases is to make use of semi-hardwood

sun and the potting mixture maintained moist, but never wet. When the cutting starts to sprout a fair number of new top leaves, showing that it has taken root, it can be uncovered and potted on in a 10 cm (4 in) pot containing peat-based mixture.

SEMI-HARDWOOD AND HEELED CUTTINGS

(11) Take your semi-hardwood cuttings by selecting 20 cm (8 in) long side-shoots of the current year's growth and cut close to the main stem. Remove the lower leaves and trim the shoot under the lowest leaf node. Trim off the upper part of the shoot so that you have a prepared cutting about 10 cm (4 in) long.

(12) A heeled cutting can be taken by making a slanting cut into the main branch from

which you wish to remove a side-shoot. The cutting is then prepared in the same way as a semi-hardwood cutting, except that of course you must not trim the lower half.

(13) Both semi-hardwood and heeled cuttings need the protection of a garden frame, greenhouse or a propagating tray in your house if they are to be rooted successfully. Once the cuttings have been taken, fill a 7.5 cm (3 in) pot with peat-based cutting mixture and, after having dipped the cuttings in the appropriate hormone rooting agent, insert up to five of them one-third of their length around the sides of the pot. If you have more cuttings, a 12.5 cm (5 in) pot will take ten, while a standard sized propagating tray will take about three dozen.

cuttings taken in summer. A semi-hardwood cutting is taken from a shoot of the current year's growth, which is firm and woody towards its base, but is soft and still growing at its topmost end. These particular cuttings are taken in mid- and late summer, depending on the growing conditions and the summer weather. Should you live where the summer can be hot, you can take the cuttings in early summer.

There are also some shrubs, such as the *Pyracantha* (Firethorn) and skimmia, which root better if the semi-hardwood cuttings are taken with a 'heel'. Heeled cuttings are simply ordinary stem cuttings with a portion of the main branch or

(14) All these cuttings need a humid atmosphere, which is achieved by covering the containers. The propagating pot or tray should then be placed in a shaded garden frame or greenhouse. Warmth is vital, but the scorching rays of the sun have to be avoided. The best rooting conditions are provided by an electric propagator.

Under average conditions most cuttings will have taken root in three weeks, by which time you should attempt to acclimatize the cuttings to drier and colder conditions. Start by making a few holes in the polythene bag, or by opening the ventilator on the propagator cover. In the following week, increase the ventilation, and a week later remove the cover completely. All this period keep the cuttings out of strong sunlight.

(15) About seven weeks from the time you took the cuttings, you can separate them gently and plant them in individual 10 cm (4 in) pots containing peat-based potting mixture so that their lower leaves are just above the surface of the compost. After three or four weeks the root will completely fill the pot. At this time the hardiest of such new shrubs can be planted in their final positions in the garden. If the shrubs are known to be tender, transplant them instead to larger pots and keep them in the greenhouse or garden frame until the more favourable weather of spring.

LAYERING

(16) The best branches or shoots for layering are the ones which have grown in the current year. Deciduous shrubs are best layered in autumn or winter; evergreen shrubs should be layered in autumn or spring. First, fork over lightly the surface of the soil around the shrub. Then, choose a suitable flexible branch and bend it down until it touches the soil about 25 cm (10 in) from the tip. Remove the leaves from the branch where it meets the soil and wound the underside of the branch by cutting a sliver of bark with a knife. Dig a hole 10 cm (4 in) deep under the wounded part of the branch and half fill with peat-based cuttings mixture. Next, press

older wood at the lower end.

Layering is a method of propagating shrubs outdoors and does away with the need for a garden frame or greenhouse. It is based on the knowledge that when a shoot is cut or damaged, it is likely to produce roots if it comes in contact with the soil.

Serpentine layering is similar to ordinary layering except that it is the technique which is normally used to propagate climbing plants.

The most common and simplest form of propagation is root division. The roots of most herbaceous plants can be divided into pieces in spring and replanted. You can also increase shrubs such as ceratostigma, hypericum, kerria, pachysandra and rubus by dividing their roots in winter or early spring.

the wounded part of the branch into the hole and bend the branch upwards to form a right angle at the wound. Peg the branch to the soil with a hoop of galvanized wire and tie the upper part of the branch to a bamboo cane which should be inserted into the soil for support. Fill the hole with compost and press firm. The layered area must be watered in dry spells.

(17) After a year, the pegged branch should be growing noticeably, showing that it has taken root. You can then sever it from the parent shrub with secateurs, and after lifting it with a good ball of soil around its roots, plant it in its new position.

SERPENTINE LAYERING

(18) Serpentine layering is carried out at the same time as ordinary layering, using long trailing shoots which have grown during the current year. Bend a shoot to the ground and where it touches the soil make a 10 cm (4 in) hole beneath. Wound the shoot at this point in the same way as with ordinary layering and peg the shoot in the hole with a hoop of galvanized wire. Next, fill the hole with peat-based cuttings mixture and firm with your fingers. The following two pairs of leaves should be left above ground. Then repeat as before. You can continue in this way for the entire length of the shoot. About a year later, check that each section has taken root. Cut through the individual sections with secateurs, lift with a good ball of soil and plant in a new position.

ROOT DIVISION

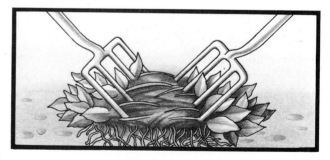

(19) With root division, lift the herbaceous plant or shrub (at least three years old) with a fork and divide the roots into several good sized pieces, each with plenty of roots. With some shrubs the division can be done by tearing the roots apart with your hands or by using secateurs. However, with the majority of herbaceous plants, you will need a couple of garden forks, back to back, to prize the roots apart. The pieces of roots can then be planted in their new positions. With smaller plants such as the primrose and most rockery plants, root division is easily done with your fingers. In some cases it may not even be necessary to dig up the entire plant first.

Vegetables

For a lot of people gardening has come to mean growing
vegetables, and, apart from the money that can be saved,
there is one great incentive—the sheer satisfaction of being
able to provide some of one's own food, of being able to
say, 'I grew that...'

Getting the best possible vegetables from a limited amount of space calls for some very careful planning. There are four basic steps you should aim to follow.

Step one is to prepare the soil thoroughly. The time for digging is in late autumn or early winter if you want to be able to sow in spring. With heavy soils, the earlier you dig the better so that they have sufficient time to be weathered by rain and frost to a sufficiently friable (crumbled) texture for seed sowing.

Step two is to make the soil suitable for particular vegetables, as there are three basic groups of vegetables with different requirements. In the first group there are the root crops, such as beetroot, carrot, parsnip, potato, swede and turnip. These vegetables need the addition of a general fertilizer to the soil before sowing. In the second group are the 'greens', or brassicas, vegetables such as broccoli, Brussels sprouts, cabbage, cauliflower and spinach. The soil for these vegetables should be limed if necessary in winter. Your best plan is to make a simple soil test first. Aim at pH 6.5 to 6.8. The area for brassicas should also be given a top dressing of general fertilizer before sowing or planting. In the third group are all the other vegetables such as asparagus, beans, celery, cucumber, leek, lettuce, marrow, onion, peas, radish, sweetcorn and tomato. The soil for these vegetables should be enriched with compost when you do the autumn or winter digging and top dressed with general fertilizer before sowing or planting. The importance of plenty of good compost cannot be overstressed if you want to be certain of success with vegetables.

The three groups of vegetables, with their varying demands on the soil, mean that we have to use some form of crop rotation to give the soil a chance to recover. Crop rotation also helps to prevent a build-up of disease. This is the ideal, but in the majority of gardens today proper rotation is impossible because of the lack of space. However, by careful planning, you should be able to avoid growing the same group of vegetables in the same position two years running.

Right: A large, efficient vegetable garden in midsummer. On view are perpetual straw-berries, seedlings and carrots, with separate plots for peas, potatoes, onions and brassicas. Previous page: A small but productive plot.

Above: Red and green peppers.

Step three is to sow and plant at the correct time. Forget what it says on the back of the seed packet. You alone can determine your local conditions. If the weather is cold and wet in spring, wait a while. You will gain nothing by attempting to sow in unsuitable conditions. There is an old gardening adage that you should not sow seed outdoors until you see the weeds growing. When sowing, make allowances for the texture of your soil. A depth of 2.5 cm (1 in) may be all right in light soil, but on heavy land 1 cm ($\frac{1}{2}$ in) will be safer if you want the seeds to germinate. You will also make life easier for the young plants by sowing thinly so that they are not competing for moisture, light and air. In any case, always thin out in plenty of time before the plants become drawn and weakened.

Step four is to get the best possible productivity out of a limited area by a technique called intercropping. Some vegetables mature in weeks, while others take months. So you can grow fast-maturing crops between the rows of slower-maturing vegetables. Between rows of beans (broad, French and runner) you can grow lettuces, radishes and beetroots. Broad beans can also be intercropped with Brussels sprouts. The brassicas can be intercropped with lettuce, beetroot and dwarf beans. Between rows of celery you can have dwarf beans, peas and lettuce.

A second example of getting maximum productivity is called catch-cropping. This is the practice of growing a fast-maturing vegetable in soil that is empty for a short period between the harvesting of one crop and the sowing and planting of another. An example of catch-cropping is the sowing of carrots in early spring on ground which will later be planted in early summer with cabbages. Radishes are a good catch crop since they mature in six weeks or so from sowing. Accurate timing is vital. If you sow the catch crop too late, it will not have matured in time for you to plant the main crop.

98

Not all seeds can be sown directly out of doors. Some, such as celery and tomatoes, have to be sown indoors and planted outdoors once the risk of frost has passed. Some vegetable plants too can be raised by sowing the seeds directly into peat pots or peat blocks. In areas with poor growing conditions, this practice also assures better yields from crops such as brassicas.

BRASSICAS

BROCCOLI
Sprouting broccoli—calabrese (or green), purple and white varieties
Sowing to harvest time: 12 to 16 weeks for calabrese; 40 weeks for purple and white varieties.
Yield: Calabrese, up to 0.9 kg (2 lb) per plant; other varieties, average 0.45 kg (1 lb) per plant.
Climate preferred: Cool temperate to sub-tropical.
Aspect: Open, but sheltered from strong winds.
Soil: Heavy, firm and rich in organic matter.

Broccoli is closely related to the cauliflower, but it is very much easier to grow. It can withstand more heat *and* more cold than the cabbage. If you are growing calabrese, make use of the latest hybrids which mature rapidly and give huge yields.

Sowing and planting
The seed should be sown thinly in rows 1.3 cm (½ in) deep. *Calabrese* (green sprouting broccoli): sow in mid- or late spring and thin early to prevent the plants from being weakened through over-crowding. When the seedlings are 7.5 cm (3 in) high, move them to their permanent positions with 45 cm (18 in) between the plants and 60 cm (2 ft) between the rows. Before setting the plants in their final positions, give the plot a dressing of vegetable fertilizer at the rate of 135 gm per sq m (4 oz per sq yd). When transplanting, fill the holes with water. Allow to drain. Then set the plants 2.5 cm (1 in) deeper in the holes than they were in the seed bed. Finally firm the soil around the plants with your fingers. *Purple sprouting broccoli* is the hardiest of the broccolis and grows well in cold areas and on heavy clay soils. Sow the seeds as before in late spring and transplant the seedlings when they are 7.5 cm (3 in) high to produce a crop from early winter to late spring, depending on the

BRASSICAS

(1) As brassicas require a well-consolidated soil, prepare the plot several months in advance of planting by giving it a dressing of lime if necessary. Get the seed bed ready for sowing by treading the soil really firm at a time when it is sufficiently dry so that it will not stick to your boots. Apply a top dressing of general fertilizer at the rate of 135 gm per sq m (4 oz per sq yd) and rake the soil to produce a fine, crumbly surface.

(2) Make a shallow drill for seed sowing by using the back of the head of the rake and sow the seed very thinly. Insert a label in the soil with the name of the crop, the variety and date of sowing. Then gently rake sufficient soil back into the drill to cover the seeds. Dust along the drill with soil insecticide to prevent root fly. Finally rake the soil carefully to remove all trace of footprints.

variety. *White sprouting broccoli*, if sown at the same time, will give a crop between early and late spring, depending on the variety. All broccoli requires regular hoeing of the soil to keep down weeds. The soil should also be kept well watered in dry spells. Feed with nitrochalk at the rate of 34 gm per sq m (1 oz per sq yd) in rings around the plants four weeks after transplanting. With purple and white sprouting broccoli, draw up soil around the stems in autumn to prevent their being toppled by winter winds. Alternatively provide each plant with a bamboo stake.

Pests and diseases
Birds (especially pigeons), aphids, caterpillars, club root and root fly.

Harvesting
The 'spears' should be cut when they are small and not too far developed: at a point just before the flower buds have opened. Cut the main centre spear first and then all the side spears. With the calabrese hybrids, the centre spear usually takes the form of a sizeable head, not unlike that of a cauliflower. Keep cutting the spears as they develop and never let the plant flower or the production of fresh spears will stop. Store by freezing.

BRUSSELS SPROUTS
Sowing to harvest time: 28 to 36 weeks, depending on the variety.
Yield: 1 kg (2 lb) of sprouts to a plant.
Climate preferred: Cool temperate.
Aspect: Open, but sheltered from strong winds.
Soil: Heavy, firm and rich in organic matter.

Brussels sprouts are an excellent green crop for the winter months and freshly picked sprouts have an especially good flavour. It is worth paying a bit more for the seed of the modern small hybrid varieties, better suited to the smaller garden.

(3) As soon as the seedlings can be handled easily, thin them out to leave the remainder about 2.5 cm (1 in) to prevent their becoming 'leggy'.

(4) When transplanting, make a hole with a

trowel. Then, if the soil is dry, fill the hole with water and allow to drain.

(5) Next, puff some Calomel dust (taking care not to breathe in any as it is very poisonous) into each hole to prevent club root, before planting each seedling at the correct depth (refer to the individual brassica concerned).
Summer cabbages and summer cauliflowers are best sown indoors in a seed tray containing peat-based potting mixture. You can either keep the tray indoors, or, better still, place it in a garden frame until the plants are sufficiently large to be set out in their final positions. If the plants are kept indoors, it will be necessary to harden them

Sowing and planting
Sow the seed 1.3 cm (½ in) deep outdoors between early and late spring, depending on the variety and the location. When the seedlings are 15 cm (6 in) high, they are ready to be transplanted. But first firm the soil with your feet; give it a dressing of general fertilizer at the rate of 135 gm per sq m (4 oz per sq yd); and rake it level. When transplanting, set the plants in holes 60 cm (2 ft) apart each way. (The holes should have been previously filled with water, and allowed to drain.) The lowest pair of leaves on each plant should touch the soil, which should be firmed with your fingers. Hoe the soil around the plants regularly and water well in dry spells. Six weeks after transplanting feed with nitrochalk at the rate of 34 gm per sq m (1 oz per sq yd) in rings around the plants and hoe in lightly. In windy areas draw soil up the stems, or tie the stems to bamboo canes in autumn to prevent the plants being felled by the wind. Loose soil and unsteady plants cause the sprouts to become 'brown'.

Pests and diseases
Aphids, birds (sparrows eat seedlings; pigeons go for the mature plants), caterpillars, club root, flea beetles and root fly.

Harvesting
Start to pick the sprouts at the bottom of the stem when they are still tightly closed. Store by freezing.

CABBAGE
winter, spring or summer
Sowing to harvest time: summer and winter varieties, 20 to 35 weeks; spring varieties, 25 weeks.
Yield: 1 to 2 kg (1 to 4½ lb) a plant.
Climate preferred: Cool temperate.
Aspect: Open.
Soil: Ordinary, well-drained and firm.

---

off before transplanting by placing the seed tray outdoors in the shelter of a warm wall for a few days.

(6) If you want top-quality Brussels sprouts, calabrese and cauliflowers, sow three seeds to each peat block or 5 cm (2 in) peat pot containing peat-based mixture and thin out to leave just one seedling to each pot. The pots have to be kept indoors, in a greenhouse, or in a cold frame until they are ready for planting direct into the soil.

Young brassicas require plenty of water if they are to make steady progress. You can either apply water from a watering can or by using a sprinkler. If you use the latter, make sure that you leave it on long enough to soak the soil. It is pointless and harmful simply to wet the top few centimetres (inches). In light soil which dries out rapidly, the maximum benefit from watering can be achieved by setting out the plants in a shallow trench.

(7) Hoeing is the best way of keeping down weeds. The action of the hoe also breaks down the surface into a crumbly texture which does not lose moisture so rapidly as soil which

Cabbages are one of the easiest vegetables to grow in areas where the climate is generally unfavourable. By making use of the modern smaller varieties, and by planting a combination of spring, summer and winter cabbages in succession, it is possible to have fresh cabbage all year.

Sowing and planting

The seed should be sown thinly in rows 1.3 cm (1 in) deep. *Winter varieties* (including red cabbages and the crinkly leaved savoys): Sow outdoors in late spring and transplant during early summer. *Spring varieties*: Sow in mid- and late summer and transplant in early or mid-autumn. *Summer varieties*: Either sow indoors (or under glass) in late winter and plant out in early mid-spring or sow outdoors in mid-spring and transplant in late spring or early summer. The seedlings should be transferred to their final positions when they have six leaves. About two weeks prior to transplanting, top dress the soil with general fertilizer at the rate

Right: Plant cabbages so that they will just touch each other when mature.

of 135 gm per sq m (4 oz per sq yd). When transplanting, firm the soil around the plants thoroughly and water as necessary if the weather is dry. Allow 30 to 45 cm (1 to 1½ ft) between the plants, depending on the variety and type. About six weeks or so after planting out apply a top dressing of general fertilizer at the rate of 34 gm per sq m (1 oz per sq yd) around the plants and hoe in lightly. Keep the soil surface free from weeds by regular hoeing and water regularly in dry spells as cabbages grown in drought conditions have a poor flavour.

Pests and diseases

Aphids, caterpillars, club root and root fly.

Harvesting

Cut fresh from the garden as required.

---

has been allowed to form a crust. When hoeing, push the blade into the soil so that it stirs the surface and does the minimum amount of damage to shallow roots.

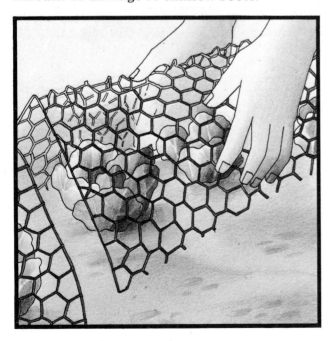

(8) **Birds can do enormous damage to seedlings and mature brassicas. The remedy is to cover the crop with netting before the problem arises.**

(9) **With Brussels sprouts, remove the lower leaves as they turn yellow to make harvesting easier. The sprouts should be picked, starting at ground level and working your way up to the top of the plant.**

102

CAULIFLOWER

Sowing to harvest time: 18 to 24 weeks for summer and autumn varieties; 40 weeks for winter varieties.

Yield: 1 kg (2 lb) per plant.

Climate preferred: Cool temperate to sub-tropical.

Aspect: Open, but sheltered from cold winds.

Soil: Rich, fertile loam, but sandy soils are suitable if plenty of organic material has been incorporated during the winter.

'Summer' cauliflowers are in season from mid-summer to early autumn; 'autumn' varieties from mid-autumn to early winter and 'winter' cauliflowers from mid-winter to early spring. Consider growing one of the Australian varieties, which are dwarf growing and which produce superb little firm white heads in autumn.

Sowing and planting

Summer varieties should be sown indoors in mid-winter and set outside in mid-spring to provide a midsummer crop. *Autumn varieties* should be sown outdoors in mid- and late spring and transplanted towards the end of early summer. *Winter varieties* should be sown outdoors in late spring and transplanted in midsummer. The seed should be sown 1.3 cm ($\frac{1}{2}$ in) deep, and the seedlings are ready to transplant when they have six leaves. Two weeks before transplanting give the soil a top dressing of general fertilizer at the rate of 135 gm per sq m (4 oz per sq yd). Set the plants in holes which have been previously filled with water and allowed to drain, 60 cm (2 ft) apart each way. The little plants should sit at the same level as they did in the seed bed. The secret of success with cauliflowers is to keep them well watered. If you let them wilt during the first few days after transplanting, they are unlikely later to produce tight heads. A top dressing of nitrochalk at the rate of 34 gm per sq m (1 oz per sq yd) should be applied in rings around the plants at four weeks and again at eight weeks after setting them out to improve the quality and flavour of the curds. Summer varieties should have a few leaves bent

BEANS and PEAS

(1) **Broad beans can be sown in seed trays in late winter or early spring and the seed trays kept in a cold frame before setting the plants out in the vegetable plot in mid-spring. A similar method of raising the plants can be used with runner beans. However, these should not be sown until late spring. In both cases, sow only 18 seeds in each standard sized seed tray so that you will get sturdy plants with good root systems.**

(2) **To sow broad beans, dig a shallow trench 23 cm (9 in) wide and about 5 cm (2 in) deep. Then place the seeds in two rows with 15 cm (6 in) between the seeds and 23 cm (9 in) between the rows. After labelling and marking the position of the beans, draw soil over them with a rake. In light and sandy soil, the beans can be covered to 5 cm (2 in). However, with cold and heavy soil, it is better to cover to 2.5 cm (1 in) to ensure the best possible germination.**

over the curds to protect them from the sun and to keep them snowy white. With winter varieties a similar measure protects the curds from the yellowing effect of frost and snow.

Pests and diseases
Aphids, caterpillars, club root, flea beetles and root fly.

Harvesting
Cut cauliflowers while they are still small and tender. Summer and autumn varieties are at their best if cut in the morning with the dew still on the curds. In frosty weather, winter cauliflowers are best cut at midday. Cauliflowers hung upside down in a shed or garage remain in good condition for two weeks. Otherwise, store by freezing.

BEANS AND PEAS

BROAD BEAN
Sowing to harvest time: 16 weeks for spring sowings; 28 weeks for autumn sowings.
Yield: 5 kg (11 lb) to a 3 m (10 ft) double row. Dwarf varieties, 2 kg (4½ lb) to a single row.
Climate preferred: Cool temperate.
Aspect: Open
Soil: Ordinary, but well-drained.

Broad beans are one of the easiest vegetables to grow and you have a choice of three main types. There are the longpod varieties, recognizable by their long, narrow pods. These are the best choice for hardiness, top yields and early crops. Next there are the Windsor varieties, characterized by their shorter and wider pods. These are the best choice for flavour and later crops, but they cannot be sown in autumn. Finally there are the dwarf varieties, which have short pods and dwarf, bushy growth. These are ideal for small vegetable plots and in areas which are exposed to strong winds. Dwarf varieties are normally grown in single rows, unlike the others which are usually grown in double rows. Dwarf beans will give smaller crops than the normal-sized varieties.

(3) Broad beans are very susceptible to attack by blackfly. However, you can lessen the likelihood of a heavy infestation by pinching out the growing tips once the pods have started to form. This also has the benefit of encouraging the beans to develop. Unfortunately in many areas it will still be necessary to resort to using an insecticide.

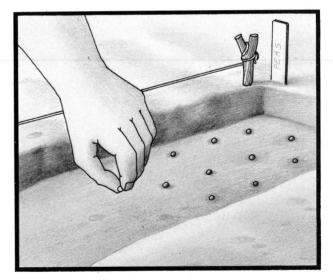

(4) Sowing peas calls for a special technique. Make a flat-bottomed trench 15 cm (6 in) wide and 5 cm (2 in) deep in light soil, 2.5 cm (1 in) deep in heavy soil. The seeds are then placed by hand in three staggered rows so that each seed is approximately 7.5 cm (3 in) apart from its neighbours. Subsequent drills of peas should be a distance apart equal to eventual height of the particular variety. After labelling and marking the position of the drills, draw soil over the seed with a rake.

Sowing and planting

The soil should be dug over in late autumn or early winter and enriched with compost. About a week before sowing, give the soil a dressing of vegetable fertilizer at the rate of 135 gm per sq m (4 oz per sq yd). In areas where the winters are mild, the long pod varieties can be sown in late autumn, 5 cm (2 in) deep with 15 cm (5 in) between the seeds. A second row should be sown just 23 cm (9 in) away. Subsequent sets of double rows should be 60 cm (2 ft) apart. If possible cover with cloches over the winter. All varieties can also be sown in early and mid-spring. Keep the plants well supplied with water and free from weeds.

Pests and diseases

Aphids (especially blackfly), botrytis (grey mould) and slugs.

Harvesting

Pick the pods while the scar on each bean in the shell is green or white (*not* black) for top flavour. Store by freezing.

FRENCH BEAN
(also called kidney and string bean)

Sowing to harvest time: 10 to 14 weeks.
Yield: dwarf varieties, 3 kg (6½ lb) to a 3 m (10 ft) row; climbing varieties, 4½ kg (10 lb) to a 3 m (10 ft) row.
Climate preferred: Cool temperate to subtropical.
Aspect: Open and sunny.
Soil: Light and well-drained.

French beans are at their best when they are picked small and tender, and this is just one of the many advantages of growing your own crop.

Sowing and planting

The soil should be dug over in late autumn or early winter and enriched with compost. About a week before sowing, top dress the soil with vegetable fertilizer at the rate of 135 gm per sq m (4 oz per sq yd) and rake this in. If you have cloches, you can start sowing in mid-spring in rows 5 cm (2 in) deep and 60 cm (2 ft) apart for dwarf varieties,

(5) Medium and tall varieties of peas (and also broad beans) should be boxed in with either plastic or wire netting secured to strong stakes and wires to provide adequate support.

(6) Climbing beans are best given the support of poles or bamboo canes inserted into the soil so that they form an inverted V shape. It is important that such a structure is very strong since the crop will be of considerable weight. Runner beans can also be grown up plastic netting held by sturdy posts.

90 cm (3 ft) apart for the taller varieties. The seeds should be spaced 7.5 cm (3 in) apart and later thinned or transplanted to 20 to 30 cm (8 to 12 in) apart in the row. Without cloches you can make successional sowings from late spring to early summer. However, if cloches were available, you could also make a sowing in midsummer to provide an autumn crop. The cloches are necessary for covering the crop in mid-autumn. Climbing varieties will need the support of plastic bean netting or sticks. The soil should be hoed regularly to keep it free from weeds and open to air and moisture. Water well in dry spells and spray the flowers gently with water in the evening to encourage pods to form.

Pests and diseases
Aphids, botrytis, capsids and slugs (a particular problem with seedlings).

Harvesting
The pods are ready for picking at about 10 cm (4 in) long when they snap easily if bent. Do not wait until the beans bulge visibly in the pods. Harvest several times a week if necessary so that the plants will continue to crop for six to eight weeks. Store by freezing.

RUNNER BEAN
Sowing to harvest time: 12 to 16 weeks.
Yield: climbing varieties, 18 kg (40 lb) to a 3 m (10 ft) row; dwarf varieties, 8 kg (17½ lb) to a 3 m (10 ft) row.
Climate preferred: Cool temperate to subtropical.
Aspect: Open, sunny and sheltered from winds.
Soil: Moist with plenty of added compost. Heavy clay and sandy soils are unsuitable.

The runner bean gives the best value of any vegetable crop. It is also the most attractive: there are varieties with scarlet, pink and white flowers and all have handsome green leaves. The most common varieties are climbers which can produce pods up to 50 cm (20 in) long. However, there are also dwarf runner beans with pods just 20 cm (8 in) long which are most suitable in small gardens or in cold, windy situations.

Sowing and planting
The position for runner beans should be prepared in winter by digging over an area 45 cm (18 in) wide and one spit deep and incorporating a thick layer of compost in the bottom. In mild areas the seeds can be sown outdoors at the end of spring, 5 cm (2 in) deep and 23 cm (9 in) apart with 38 cm (15 in) between the first and second row. At each 23 cm (9 in) interval two seeds should be placed to allow for losses and the weaker seedlings remaining should be removed soon after germination. Subsequent double rows of beans should be 1.5 m (5 ft) away. In cold districts it is best to sow the seeds indoors or in a cold frame in late spring. Climbing beans will require stout bamboo canes or poles for support. Dwarf beans need the support of short twigs inserted at intervals along the row. Keep the soil hoed and free from weeds. Copious watering is essential in dry spells, and the flowers should be sprayed gently in the evenings during dry spells to encourage pods to form. A thick moisture-retaining and weed-suppressing layer of compost or moist peat can be put down around the plants in midsummer. In late midsummer and again in late summer, feed the plants with liquid fertilizer. Once the plants reach the full height of their supports, cut their tops to stop further growth.

Pests and diseases
Seeds may be eaten by millepedes and slugs. Mature plants may be attacked by aphids, capsids and botrytis (in wet summers).

Harvesting
Pick the pods when they are young and tender and do not wait until they are long and 'stringy' with the seeds bulging in the pods. By picking regularly, you should be able to harvest fresh for more than six weeks. Store the surplus by freezing or salting.

PEAS
including petit pois and sugar peas (mangetout)
Sowing to harvest time: 32 weeks for autumn sowings; 11 to 16 weeks for spring sowings.
Yield: 3 to 7 kg (6½ to 15 lb) to a 3 m (10 ft) row, depending on the variety and whether it is dwarf or tall.
Climate preferred: Cool temperate.
Aspect: Open
Soil: Well-drained and rich in organic matter.

The common peas come in two distinct types. There are round varieties which are very handy and the quickest of all peas to mature. Then there are the wrinkle-seeded peas which are considerably sweeter and heavier cropping. The French varieties of wrinkle-seeded pea are known as petit pois. Finally there are the sugar pea varieties or, as they are appropriately called in France, mangetout which are eaten pods and all.

Sowing and planting
The soil should be enriched with compost during the digging of autumn or early winter and limed if necessary, since peas prefer an alkaline soil. About a week before sowing give the soil a dressing of vegetable fertilizer at the rate of 100 gm per sq m (3 oz per sq yd) and rake the soil backwards and forwards to make it fine and crumbly. To obtain a crop of peas in late spring and early summer, you should sow a round variety in either mid- or late autumn and cover with cloches. For peas in early and midsummer, sow an early variety of wrinkle-seeded pea in early or mid-spring. For peas in late summer, sow a maincrop wrinkled variety in mid- or late spring. This is also the time to sow both petit pois and sugar peas. For peas in early autumn, sow a wrinkled variety in early or midsummer. The technique of sowing peas is the same for all varieties. Newly sown seeds, unless covered with cloches, should be protected with plastic netting or wire netting guards. Hoe the soil regularly to keep it open and crumbly and to keep it free from weeds. When the pea plants are 15 cm (6 in) high, insert twiggy branches along the outer sides of the drills to provide support. Dwarf varieties will not require any further assistance, but medium and tall varieties, especially those of sugar peas, will require plastic or wire netting erected close to the plants for support. When the flowers appear, spray in the evenings with an insecticide to combat the pea moth and so prevent maggoty peas. As soon as the pods form, top dress the soil on either side of the plants with vegetable fertilizer at the rate of 34 gm per sq m (1 oz per sq yd) and hoe in lightly. Water well during dry spells to swell the pods.

Pests and diseases
Aphids, birds and pea moths.

Harvesting
Moving upwards from the bottom of the plants, pick the pods when they appear well filled. The sugar peas should be picked when the pods are fleshy, but before the shape of the peas can be seen in the pods. Store by freezing.

ROOT CROPS

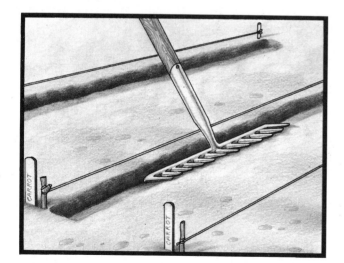

(1) Make the drill for seed sowing by securing a garden line at either side of the vegetable plot. Then, using the line as a guide, make the drill by pressing the back of the head of a rake into the soil to the required depth. The drill should then be labelled and marked at both ends with small sticks.

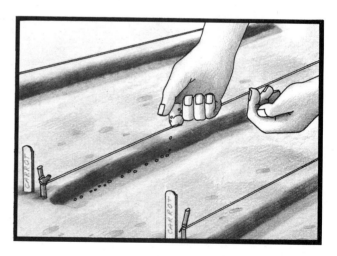

(2) When sowing seeds, it is often better to place the larger seeds by hand rather than shake them out of the packet. With the smaller seeds, shake a few into the palm of one hand and then, taking a pinch of seeds, place them in the drill with the fingers of the other. The extra effort at this point will save you the considerable labour later in thinning out the seedlings. Finally, gently draw soil over the seeds with a rake.

ROOT CROPS

CARROT

Sowing to harvest time: 12 to 14 weeks, early varieties; 18 weeks, main crop.
Yield: early varieties, 2 kg (4½ lb) to a 3 m (10 ft) row; maincrop, 4 kg (9 lb) to a 3 m (10 ft) row.
Climate preferred: Cool temperate to subtropical.
Aspect: Open and sunny, or partial shade.
Soil: Deep and light, but any soil can be made suitable.

Many people are put off growing carrots in the mistaken belief that sandy soil is required. There are carrots to suit all soils. Round and short-rooted kinds are the best choice for stony soil or clay. Stump-rooted varieties will suit the majority of soils, while those long-rooted kinds are best on sandy soils or deep, light loam.

Sowing and planting

Carrots should be grown on soil which has been well-prepared for a previous crop. Otherwise the soil should be dug deeply in autumn or winter and top dressed with vegetable fertilizer at the rate of 135 gm per sq m (4 oz per sq yd) about two weeks before sowing. Early varieties can be sown under cloches in early spring and at fortnightly intervals to mid-spring. Sowings of maincrop varieties can begin in mid-spring and continue at intervals until midsummer. Although carrots are described as early, this simply means that they are faster maturing and in fact they can be sown at intervals right up to midsummer to produce lots of delicious little carrots. Before sowing, rake the soil to make it fine and crumbly. The drills should be just 5 mm (¼ in) deep and dusted lightly before sowing with soil insecticide as a precaution against carrot fly. The seed should be sown as thinly as possible to cut down on the need for thinning later. If you wish to avoid this chore, use pelleted seed and place the pellets at 2.5 cm (1 in) intervals. Cover the drills with sifted soil and firm the surface with the flat head of a rake. Subsequent drills of early varieties should be 20 cm (8 in) apart, while the maincrop carrots should be 30 cm (12 in) apart. Thin out the seedlings, as soon as they are large enough to handle, to 5 cm (2 in) apart and later 10 cm (4 in) apart. The second thinnings will

(3) In some areas where flea beetles and carrot fly are a problem, the seed drills can be dusted with a seed dressing. Alternatively the seedlings can be dusted with an insecticide.

(4) The thinning of seedlings should be done as early as possible to enable the plants to make speedy and strong growth without too much competition for light and air. Thinning should be a progressive job and done gradually until the plants are the correct distance apart. Try not to bruise the seedling leaves as the resultant scent is thought to be a lure to certain insect pests.

Left: Perfect, tender carrots.

provide usable little carrots. Hoe frequently to keep the soil crumbly and free from weeds.

Pests and diseases
Aphids (leaves turn red and the plants are stunted) and carrot fly.

Harvesting
The crop can be lifted as required. Store in boxes of dry peat or by freezing.

BEETROOT
Sowing to harvest time: 12 to 18 weeks.

Yield: early varieties, 3 kg (6½ lb) to a 3 m (10 ft) row; maincrop, 4 kg (9 lb) to a 3 m (10 ft) row.
Climate preferred: Cool temperate.
Aspect: Open.
Soil: Light and fertile.

Beetroot makes a useful accompaniment to salads. As well as the dark red beets, there are golden beets and white beets, which are equally delicious.

Sowing and planting
The soil should be prepared by digging over in autumn or winter and should be top dressed with vegetable fertilizer at the rate of 135 gm per sq m (4 oz per sq yd) about two weeks before sowing. Sow the seeds very thinly 2.5 cm (1 in) deep in rows 30 cm (12 in) apart. Successional sowings can be

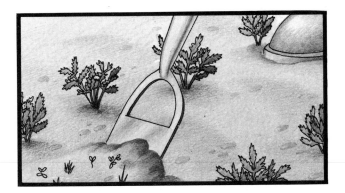

(5) Keep the soil around the plants hoed and free from weeds. The benefits of so doing are twofold: first, friable soil retains moisture better than soil which has been allowed to become baked or trodden down hard; and, secondly, by removing weeds you get rid of a potential home for pests, as well as making sure that the cultivated crop gets the maximum benefit from the soil.

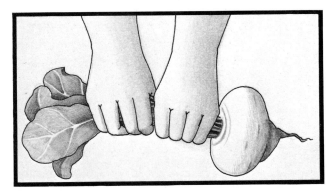

(6) Root crops such as carrots, parsnips,

salsify, swede and turnip are best gently eased out of the soil with a fork. Once the soil has dried on them it can be brushed off with your hand. The foliage growth of carrots, swedes and turnips should be removed by twisting it in a circular motion about 2.5 cm (1 in) above the root. Beetroot and summer radishes can be pulled from the soil as required.

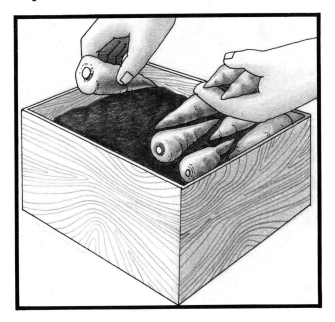

(7) The dried and clean roots can be stored in layers in boxes with dry peat between layers. The boxes can then be kept in a frost-free shed or garage until the roots are required.

made from mid-spring to early summer for a steady supply. The maincrop for winter storage should be sown in early summer. As soon as the seedlings can be handled easily, thin out to 5 cm (2 in) apart. Later thin to 10 cm (4 in) apart and use the thinnings as whole baby beets for salads. Hoe to keep down weeds, but be careful not to bruise the roots. Water when necessary to prevent the roots from splitting.

Pests and diseases
Leaf miners.

Harvesting
Lift small beets as required. The maincrop should be lifted in early mid-autumn and the dry roots stored in boxes of dried peat. Alternatively store by picking.

PARSNIP
Sowing to harvest time: 30 to 34 weeks.
Yield: 4 kg (9 lb) to a 3 m (10 ft) row.
Climate preferred: Cool temperate.
Aspect: Open and sunny.
Soil: Deep, rich, fairly light soil is ideal, but most soils are suitable with correct varieties.

There are three distinct types of parsnips. The short-rooted kinds are the best choice for stony soils or where the parsnip disease, canker, is troublesome. The intermediate varieties are a good choice for general cultivation as they offer the top yields combined with superb flavour. The long-rooted kinds are really suitable only for ideal soil and for impressing the judges at the local vegetable show.

Sowing and planting
The soil should be dug deeply in autumn or winter. Then before sowing, break down the soil with a fork, top dress with vegetable fertilizer at the rate of 135 gm per sq m (4 oz per sq yd). and rake the soil level. The seed should be sown in early or mid-spring, depending on the weather and where you live, in drills 1.3 cm (½ in) deep with 30 cm (12 in) between them. Place the seeds in clusters of three at 20 cm (8 in) intervals and later thin out to leave just one plant at each position. Hoe to keep the soil free from weeds.

Pests and diseases
Aphids, carrot fly, leaf miner and canker (roots rot; there is no cure; so grow resistant varieties).

112

Harvesting
The roots are ready for lifting when the foliage dies down in autumn. Lift as required. The roots can be left in the soil over the winter as frost improves their flavour. Or lift and store in boxes of dry peat.

SALSIFY and SCORZONERA
Sowing to harvest time: 26 to 30 weeks.
Yield: 3 kg (6½ lb) to a 3 m (10 ft) row.
Climate preferred: Cool temperate to subtropical.
Aspect: Open and sunny or partially shaded.
Soil: Any, provided it is well-drained.

Salsify, which is white-skinned, has a distinctive, somewhat fishy taste. Hence its other name: the vegetable oyster. Scorzonera, which has black skin, has a similar flavour and both vegetables make delicious additions to winter meals.

Sowing and planting
The soil for both salsify and scorzonera should be prepared by deep digging. If possible, remove any large stones which could cause the roots to fork. Two weeks before sowing (early mid-spring for salsify, late mid-spring for scorzonera) give the soil a dressing of vegetable fertilizer at the rate of 135 gm per sq m (4 oz per sq yd) and then rake the soil to make it fine and crumbly. Sow the seeds thinly in 1.3 cm (½ in) deep drills 30 cm (12 in) apart. Later thin the seedlings to 23 cm (9 in) apart in the rows. The plants should be kept well watered and free from weeds. Since the roots bleed easily if damaged by the hoe, it is a good idea to surround them with a weed-suppressing and moisture-retaining layer of moist peat.

Pests and diseases
None of any consequence.

Harvesting
In mild areas both salsify and scorzonera can be harvested throughout the winter as required. Otherwise the crop can be lifted in autumn and the roots stored in boxes of dry peat.

SWEDE
Sowing to harvest time: 20 to 24 weeks.
Yield: 5 kg (11 lb) to a 3 m (10 ft) row.
Climate preferred: Cool temperate.
Aspect: Open.
Soil: Any.

The flavour, sweet yet peppery, makes a helping of swedes a delight to look forward to, especially on the cold days of autumn and winter.

Sowing and planting

Rake the soil occupied by a previous crop and work in a dressing of vegetable fertilizer applied at the rate of 100 gm per sq m (3 oz per sq yd). In cold districts, the seed can be sown in late spring. However, in warmer areas it is best to wait until early summer or the beginning of midsummer. Sow the seed thinly in drills 1.3 cm ($\frac{1}{2}$ in) deep and 38 cm (15 in) apart. Thin the seedlings to 30 cm (12 in) apart as soon as they are large enough to handle. Keep well watered to prevent the roots from splitting.

Pests and diseases

Flea beetles, root fly and club root.

Harvesting

Swedes can be lifted from mid-autumn onwards for use as required. In mild districts the crop can be left in the ground over winter. Elsewhere the roots can be dug up, dried and stored in boxes of dry peat.

TURNIP

Sowing to harvest time: 7 to 14 weeks.
Yield: 4 kg (9 lb) to a 3 m (10 ft) row.
Climate preferred: Cool temperate.
Aspect: Open.
Soil: Any.

There are turnips in all shapes and sizes and their skin colour ranges through pure white, yellow, purple and greenish gold.

Sowing and planting

The soil for turnips should be prepared in exactly the same way as for other members of the brassica family, which may mean adding lime in winter. However, in practice turnips are usually grown on soil just vacated by a previous unrelated crop. Before sowing, the soil should be given a top dressing of vegetable fertilizer at the rate of 100 gm per sq m (3 oz per sq yd) and then raked level. The aim is to produce a seed bed which is firm yet has a fine crumbly appearance. Early turnips can be sown in succession from mid-spring onwards in drills 1.3 cm ($\frac{1}{2}$ in) deep with 38 cm (15 in) between the drills. Maincrop turnips can be sown in late summer for harvesting in mid-autumn

for storage over the winter. For 'turnip tops' sow thinly in late summer and do not thin out. Early and maincrop seedlings should be thinned initially to 7.5 cm (3 in) apart when they have developed their first rough turnip leaves. A couple of weeks later, thin again to leave the turnips 15 cm (6 in) apart. These thinnings can be eaten. Hoe to keep the soil crumbly and free from weeds. Water thoroughly if the weather is dry to prevent the roots from splitting.

Pests and diseases

Flea beetles, root fly and club root.

Harvesting

Early turnips should be lifted as required. They are at their best when about the size of a tennis ball. In mid-autumn the maincrop can be lifted, dried and stored in boxes of dry peat.

RADISH

Sowing to harvest time: summer varieties, 4 to 6 weeks; winter varieties, 10 to 12 weeks.
Yield: summer varieties, 2 kg ($4\frac{1}{2}$ lb) to a 3 m (10 ft) row; winter varieties, $4\frac{1}{2}$ kg (10 lb) to a 3 m (10 ft) row.
Climate preferred: Cool temperate.
Aspect: Open, but will tolerate some shade.
Soil: Ordinary, provided it is well-drained.

Sowing and planting

If the soil has been fed for a previous crop, no further improvement will be necessary. If not, top dress the soil with vegetable fertilizer at the rate of 70 gm per sq m (2 oz per yd) and rake the soil backwards and forwards to make it fine and crumbly. Summer varieties should be sown in succession from early spring to early summer in drills 1.3 cm ($\frac{1}{2}$ in) deep and 15 cm (6 in) apart. Sow the seed sparingly to cut out the need for thinning. If overcrowding does take place, thin the seedlings to 2.5 cm (1 in) apart. Winter varieties should be sown from late midsummer to mid late-summer in drills 23 cm (9 in) apart and later thinned to 15 cm (6 in) apart. Plenty of water is required in dry spells as fast-growing radishes become unpleasantly woody if they experience a drought.

Pests and diseases

Flea beetles and root fly.

Harvesting

Lift summer varieties while they are still young

and tender. Winter varieties can be left in the soil and lifted during winter as required, but it is better to lift them in late autumn and to store the roots in boxes of dry peat.

TUBERS

POTATO
Planting to harvest time: early varieties, 14 weeks; maincrop varieties, 20 to 22 weeks.
Yield: 6 to 10 kg (13 to 22 lb) to a 3 m (10 ft) row.
Climate preferred: Cool temperate to subtropical.
Aspect: Open.
Soil: Most soils are suitable.

There are numerous varieties of potatoes to suit all tastes. Some are waxy and ideal for salads, while others are white and floury and ideal for mashing or baking. Some of the most recent introductions are worth trying: they are more disease resistant than the old varieties and give very good yields.

Planting
The soil for potatoes should be dug over in the autumn or early winter and enriched with compost if the soil is poor. Early varieties are planted between early and mid-spring, depending on the weather and where you live. Main crop varieties are planted from mid- to late spring. A 9 m (30 ft) row or three 3 m (10 ft) rows will require $2\frac{1}{4}$ kg

POTATOES

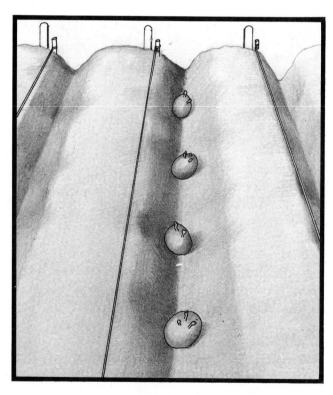

(1) Obtain your seed potatoes in late winter and place them rose end (that is the end with most of the shoots or 'eyes') uppermost in seed trays, or empty egg cartons, which should then be placed in a cool, airy, light (but not sunny) spot such as a shed or garage so that the potatoes can start to sprout. If your seed potatoes are rather large, they can be cut in pieces with several sprouts just before planting.

(2) To plant potatoes, make V-shaped drills with your spade about 13 cm (5 in) deep and 60 cm (2 ft) apart for early varieties, 75 cm (30 in) apart for main crop varieties. The early varieties need be no more than 30 cm (12 in) apart in the drills; maincrop varieties should be 38 cm (15 in) apart. The seed potatoes should be set in the drills, rose end uppermost, and first covered with a handful of peat, potting mixture or fine soil to prevent damage to the new shoots.

(5 lb) of seed potatoes. Apart from the general cultivation outlined in the step-by-step illustrations, weeds should be kept down with your hoe. The soil should also be flooded with water when the weather is dry.

Pests and diseases

Aphids, scab (action to take: grow resistant varieties), wart disease (recourse: grow resistant varieties), wireworm and blight. The last named is a disease peculiar to potatoes and it can be identified by brown markings on the leaves and the fact that the haulm (the stem and leafy tops) also collapses. The tubers develop sunken areas which are reddish brown beneath the surface. The preventative treatment for areas at risk (as not all districts suffer from blight) is to spray the foliage with Bordeaux powder from early midsummer at least three times at two-week intervals. Since blight generally affects maincrop potatoes, the solution in areas susceptible to the disease is to grow only early varieties which can be lifted from the ground before the midsummer danger period.

Harvesting

Early varieties can be lifted when the flowers wither. Maincrop varieties are lifted in early or mid-autumn when the foliage has withered. The potatoes should be allowed to dry before storing them in hessian sacks, or in slatted wooden boxes in a dark frost-free place.

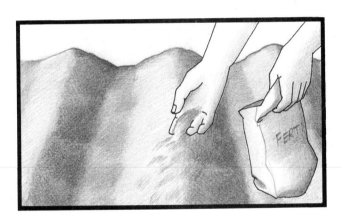

(3) The drills should then be filled in with soil so that a slight ridge is left along the drills. Next, scatter vegetable fertilizer over the drills at the rate of 135 gm per sq m (4 oz per sq yd). If there is still a risk of frost when the first shoots appear above the soil, draw a little earth over them for protection, using a hoe or spade.

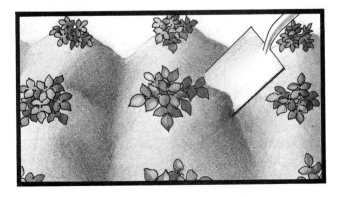

(4) When the potato shoots reach 23 cm (9 in)

high, it is time to begin the process called 'earthing up'. Fork the soil lightly between the rows, and using a spade, pile the loose soil against the stems to produce a ridge 15 cm (6 in) high. Further earthing up can be carried out as the foliage develops so that the potatoes are eventually growing in ridges.

(5) When lifting potatoes, insert your fork into the soil well away from the haulm and then lift the haulm and its roots away from the row. Give the haulm a good shake and most of the potatoes will fall away cleanly. When the haulms of maincrop potatoes have withered, cut off the stems and remove them. Then wait 10 days and lift the entire crop.

ONION FAMILY

LEEK

Sowing to harvest time: early varieties, 35 weeks; late varieties, 45 weeks.
Yield: 5 kg (11 lb) to a 3 m (10 ft) row.
Climate preferred: Cool temperate.
Aspect: Open.
Soil: Ordinary, provided that it is well-drained.

So little can go wrong with leeks that even someone new to gardening is virtually sure of success. The leek thrives in cool, wet areas where growing conditions are generally acknowledged to be poor.

Sowing and planting

Ideally the soil for leeks should have been improved with compost for a previous crop such as early potatoes. If not, enrich the soil with some well-rotted compost or peat and give it a top dressing of vegetable fertilizer at the rate of 135 gm per sq m (4 oz per sq yd) two weeks before planting. The seed should be sown outdoors in a nursery bed in a drill 1.3 cm ($\frac{1}{2}$ in) deep between early and mid-spring. The seedlings are ready for transplanting in early or midsummer when they are 20 cm (8 in) high. They should be set out in rows 30 cm (12 in) apart with 15 cm (6 in) between the plants. The plants should be kept weed-free and provided with plenty of water whenever the weather is dry. Soil can be drawn up against the stems of the plants as they develop if you wish your leeks to be well blanched.

Pests and diseases

None of any consequence.

ONION FAMILY

(1) The seed of onions should be sown very thinly 1.3 cm ($\frac{1}{2}$ in) deep in rows 30 cm (12 in) apart. Seedlings from a late summer sowing should be transplanted to 15 cm (6 in) apart with 30 cm (12 in) between the rows. Onions sown in early or mid-spring should be thinned first to 5 cm (2 in) apart and later to 15 cm (6 in) apart, maintaining 30 cm (12 in) between the rows. The thinnings can be used as 'spring onions' for salads. However, it is much better to use a special variety for this purpose. Spring onions are sown in the same way as ordinary onions except that the rows need be just 15 cm (6 in) apart and the seedlings are not thinned. Pickling onions are sown in rows 25 cm (10 in) apart and like 'spring onions' are not thinned. If onion fly is known to be troublesome, the seed drills can be dusted in spring with Calomel before sowing. Transplanted onions in spring should also be dusted with Calomel before they are set out.

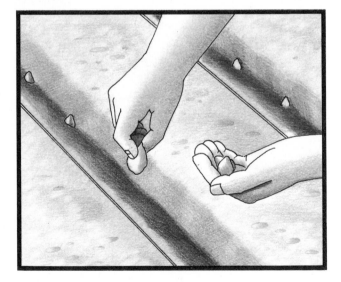

(2) To produce a crop of onions from the little bulbs called sets, each bulb should be pushed into the soil so that its neck is barely visible. The bulbs should be 15 cm (6 in) apart with 30 cm (12 in) between the rows.

Harvesting

Since leeks can remain in the soil throughout the winter months, harvest as required. To lift leeks, insert a fork fully into the soil close to the plants and gently lever them out.

ONION

bulb varieties, spring and pickling onions

Planting (or sowing) to harvest time: Onions raised from seed take 44 weeks if sown in late summer and 22 weeks if spring sown; onions raised from sets take 18 weeks; spring onions take 10 to 12 weeks; pickling onions take 22 weeks.

Yield: $3\frac{1}{2}$ kg (8 lb) of bulbs from seed or sets to a 3 m (10 ft) row and 1 kg (2 lb) of spring or pickling onions to a 3 m (10 ft) row.

Climate preferred: Cool temperate to subtropical.

Aspect: Sunny.

Soil: Well-drained, light and rich in organic matter.

Onions are an invaluable crop as they store so easily. There are also many more uses for onions than most other vegetables.

Sowing and planting

The soil for onions should be prepared by digging in plenty of compost and top dressing with vegetable fertilizer at the rate of 135 gm per sq m (4 oz per sq yd). When the soil is dry, tread it firm and then rake it carefully to produce a fine crumbly appearance. In mild districts seed can be sown in late summer to produce tiny bulbs for transplanting in early spring and to yield a crop in midsummer. Elsewhere the seed can be sown in

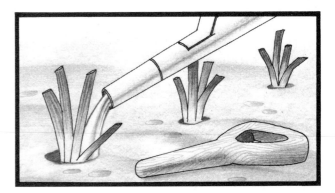

(4) **The transplanting of leeks calls for a special technique. Make 15 cm (6 in) deep holes for the plants with a dibber or stick. Next drop a single leek plant in each hole which should then be filled with water to settle soil around its roots. There is no need to fill the holes with soil.**

(3) **An additional feed of vegetable fertilizer can be given in late spring to increase the size of onion bulbs. Apply a top dressing at the rate of 70 gm per sq m (2 oz per sq yd) and hoe in lightly. All onions and leeks should be kept free from weeds by hoeing carefully along the rows. However, take care not to dig in too deeply or you will damage the roots.**

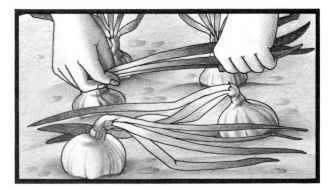

(5) **In midsummer (autumn sown) or late**

117

early or late spring to produce a late summer or early autumn crop. A variety of 'spring onion' seed should be sown as for ordinary onions, at two-weekly intervals from mid-spring to produce plenty of delicately flavoured young plants for salads. Pickling onions can also be sown in mid-spring. To produce a crop of onions the easy way you can also use those little bulbs called 'sets' which are planted in early or mid-spring.

Pests and diseases

Onion fly (but sets are generally free from attack). Birds may pull sets from the soil (the remedy is to snip off the loose skin from the necks before planting).

Harvesting

Once the foliage has shrivelled, onion bulbs can be lifted, dried and stored for future use.

SHALLOT

Planting to harvest time: 18 to 25 weeks.
Yield: $4\frac{1}{2}$ kg (10 lb) to a 3 m (10 ft) row.
Climate preferred: Cool temperate to subtropical.
Aspect: Sunny.
Soil: Well-drained nd one that is rich in organic matter.

Shallots have a milder flavour than onions and for this reason some people prefer them. They are very easy to grow and, unlike onions, each initial set forms a clump of bulbs.

Planting

The soil should be prepared in autumn or early winter by digging it over and enriching it with compost. In early part of late winter, top dress the soil with vegetable fertilizer at the rate of 70 gm

summer (spring sown or planted) bend over the tops of onions neatly to assist ripening.

necessary to dry your onions under the cover of a cold frame.

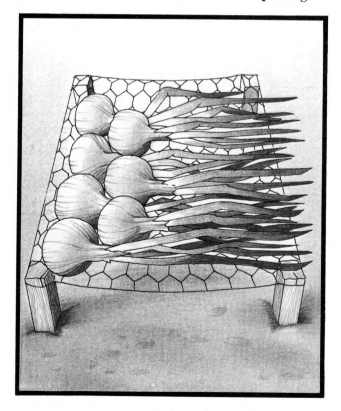

(6) **Once the leaves of onions have yellowed, the crop can be lifted and allowed to dry on a wire netting cradle several centimetres from the ground. In wet districts it may be**

(7) **Onions and shallots can be stored by plaiting them with raffia or by hanging them in plastic netting in a cool airy place.**

per sq m (2 oz per sq yd) and hoe this in. Attempt at the same time to get the soil fine and crumbly. Between late winter and early spring, push the bulbs into the soil so that their necks are barely visible. The bulbs should be 15 to 20 cm (6 to 8 in) apart. Hoe carefully to avoid damaging the bulbs and water only when absolutely necessary. In early summer scrape some soil away from the clusters of bulbs to expose them to the sun and so assist ripening.

Pests and diseases

Shallots suffer from the same pests and diseases as onions.

Harvesting

As soon as the foliage has turned yellow in early or midsummer, dig up the shallots and dry them before storing them for later use.

LETTUCE

LETTUCE

Sowing to harvest time: 10 to 14 weeks.
Yield: 10 to 30 heads, depending on the variety, to a 3 m (10 ft) row.
Climate preferred: Cool temperate.
Aspect: Open and sunny, but in summer lettuces are better in partial shade.
Soil: Well-drained and rich in humus.

There are two distinct types of lettuce: cabbage, and cos. The cabbage kinds can in turn be subdivided into butterheads, with soft floppy leaves, and crisp hearts, which have crisper leaves than the butterheads and are more resistant to summer heat and less liable to run to seed. Cos lettuces are upright and have crisp self-folding leaves. The cos type of lettuce does not run readily

LETTUCE

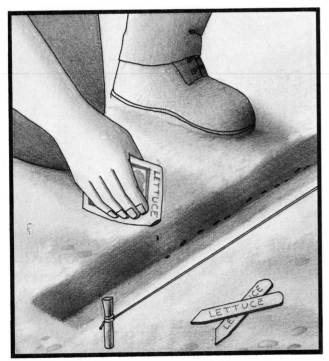

(1) The seed should be sown very thinly in short drills 1.3 cm (½ in) deep and transplanted later to 10 to 30 cm (4 to 12 in) apart, depending on the variety. It is best to raise only a few plants at a time and to sow every two weeks to ensure a continuity of supply.

(2) If you want to cut out the need for thinning, use pelleted seed and place the individual seeds in the drills 5 cm (2 in) apart with 10 to 30 cm (4 to 12 in) between the rows. When you thin out later to the required spacing, these thinnings can be used for salad. The advantage of this method of growing is that it gives faster results. Also in hot summers lettuces do not transplant easily.

After you have sown the seed fill in the drill by drawing some soil over it with a rake. Then mark the row with a label with the name of the variety and the date of sowing. If root aphids have proved troublesome, dust the seed row with soil insecticide and again when transplanting the young plants.

to seed and its leaves remain much cleaner in wet weather. There are several dwarf varieties of lettuce which are a good choice for growing in tubs and window boxes. Such small lettuces generally provide enough leaves for two people for one meal.

Sowing and planting

The soil for lettuces should be enriched if necessary with some well-rotted compost. About two weeks before sowing or planting out, the soil should be given a top dressing of vegetable fertilizer at the rate of 70 gm per sq m (2 oz per sq yd). For a summer crop, sow outdoors from the end of early spring to late midsummer to produce lettuces from early summer until the end of mid-autumn. For an early winter crop, sow a forcing variety in late summer and cover with cloches from early autumn to provide lettuces in late autumn and early winter. Forcing varieties can also be sown in the greenhouse from late summer to mid-autumn to provide lettuces from late autumn to mid-spring. For a spring crop outdoors, sow a hardy winter variety at the end of late summer or in early autumn and harvest in late spring. For lettuces in mid-spring, sow a forcing variety at the beginning of mid-autumn and cover with cloches.

Pests and diseases

Aphids, birds, millepedes, root aphids, slugs and botrytis (grey mould).

Harvesting

Lift from the garden in the early morning while the leaves are crisp and fresh.

CELERY

CELERY
Sowing to harvest time: 28 to 34 weeks.

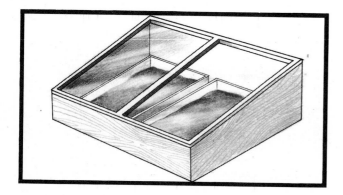

(3) In districts where the springs are cold and wet, it is worth sowing a few seeds in a small plastic seed tray containing peat-based potting mixture in late winter or early spring and standing the tray in a cold frame, greenhouse, or at the kitchen window.

(4) Lettuce plants are very vulnerable to dry

120

conditions and care must be taken when they are transplanted that the soil is sufficiently moist. This may mean adding water to the planting holes and watering the lettuces every day until they have obviously become established.

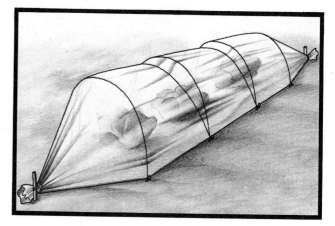

(5) Cloches are a splendid investment so far as lettuces are concerned. By covering the crop it will be protected from the birds and will mature faster, thus saving you money by having lettuces when they are expensive in the shops. Continuous tunnelling of plastic sheeting is also a worthwhile means of covering lettuce in areas where springs are wet and cold.

Yield: 6.5 kg (14 lb) to a 3 m (10 ft) row.
Climate preferred: Cool temperate to subtropical.
Aspect: Open and sunny.
Soil: Rich and well-drained, but capable of retaining moisture.

Crisp, crunchy celery stalks are a delight in salads or with cheese from late summer to spring. The stalks can also be cooked as a vegetable in soups and casseroles.

Sowing and planting
There are two types of celery: trench varieties (pink, red or white), which provide stems from autumn to spring, and the self-blanching varieties which are ready from late summer and are milder in flavour. The latter varieties have made celery growing much simpler. The plot for self-blanching varieties should be dug over in mid-spring, incorporating as much compost as possible. Trench varieties too require a special bed which should also be prepared in mid-spring. The plants should be raised by sowing the seed indoors in boxes of compost for transplanting outdoors in early or midsummer.

Pests and diseases
Celery fly (grubs cause brown blisters—spray with malathion or triclorphon), aphids, leaf miners, slugs and leaf spot (brown rusty spots on leaves and stems—spray with Bordeaux powder every two to three weeks).

Harvesting
Lift the self-blanching varieties as you need them. The trench varieties are ready about nine weeks from the start of earthing up. Remove plants from the end of the row as required, taking care to avoid disturbing neighbouring plants.

CELERY

(1) Sow the seeds indoors in early spring or mid-spring in a seed tray containing a commercial potting mixture. When the seedlings are about 2 cm (¾ in) high, transfer them to boxes of potting mixture, spaced about 7.5 cm (3 in) apart. Keep the plants under the cover of a cold frame, large cloche or greenhouse before setting them out in early or midsummer.

(2) Prepare trench for blanching varieties in mid-spring by digging out the soil 30 cm (12 in) deep and 38 cm (15 in) wide for a single row of plants, and 45 cm (18 in) wide for a double row. The trench should then have a generous amount of compost forked into the soil in the bottom. Some of the soil taken from the trench should then be returned so that the level is raised to 15 cm (6 in) from the top of the trench. The remaining soil should be used to make mounds 7.5 cm (3 in) high on either side of the trench. Finally top dress the soil in the trench with vegetable fertilizer at the rate of 135 gm per sq m (4 oz per sq yd).

121

SWEETCORN

SWEETCORN

Sowing to harvest time: 12 to 16 weeks.
Yield: At least two cobs to a plant.
Climate preferred: Cool temperate to subtropical.
Aspect: Open and sunny.
Soil: Any, if enriched with compost.

Home-grown sweetcorn is a real delight, and, with some of the most recent hybrids, remarkably easy to grow.

Right: Home-grown sweetcorn.

Sowing and planting

The soil for sweetcorn should be improved by the addition of compost during the annual digging in autumn or early winter. Then two weeks before planting top dress the soil with vegetable fertilizer at the rate of 135 gm per sq m (4 oz per sq yd). The sweetcorn plants can be raised by sowing the seeds indoors between mid-spring and late spring. Alternatively you can sow the seeds direct outdoors late spring or early summer. Two seeds should be sown together 2.5 cm (1 in) deep every 45 cm (18 in)

(3) Self-blanching varieties should be planted in a square on a specially enriched plot, so that the plants are 23 cm (9 in) apart each way. Feed regularly with liquid fertilizer.

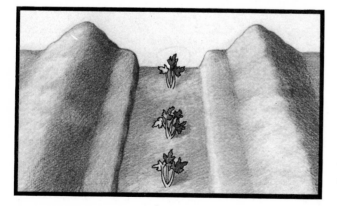

to earth up later. After you have finished planting, flood the trench with water. Every couple of weeks in mid- and late summer feed the plants with a liquid general fertilizer.

(4) Trench varieties should be spaced 25 cm (10 in) in a single row down the middle of the 38 cm (15 in) wide trench. If planting a double row in a 45 cm (18 in) wide trench, space the plants 30 cm (12 in) apart with 25 cm (10 in) between the rows. Do not stagger the rows, as setting the plants in pairs makes them easier

(5) When the trench varieties are 25 cm (10 in) high, blanching can begin. Remove any side-shoots, wrap the stems in newspaper collars, secured loosely to allow room for the hearts to develop and pile the soil in the mounds on either side of the trench against the collars.

122

along rows spaced 45 cm (18 in) apart; or in blocks, having several short rows, rather than one long row, to reduce the risk of wind damage. Once the seedlings are large enough to handle, thin to leave the strongest plant 45 cm (18 in) apart. Since the roots of sweetcorn are very close to the surface, a moisture-retaining and weed-suppressing layer of peat is beneficial. Do not hoe between the plants; better to let the weeds grow rather than destroy the roots of the sweetcorn. Flood the soil around the plants in dry weather.

Harvesting

The ripe cobs should be twisted free from the plants. Store by freezing.

Pests and diseases

None of any consequence.

ASPARAGUS

ASPARAGUS

Planting to harvest time: The plants crop in the second year from crowns.
Yield: 2 kg (4½ lb) to a 3 m (10 ft) row, but the yield increases with the age of the plants.
Aspect: Open, sunny and, if possible, on a southerly slope.
Climate preferred: Cool temperate to subtropical.

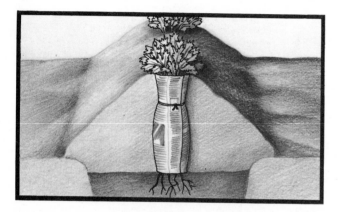

(6) In early autumn, complete earthing up so that only the top tuft of foliage is showing. In cold districts it may be necessary to protect the exposed leaves with straw or bracken during late autumn and winter.

SWEETCORN

(1) Sweetcorn plants can be raised by sowing

the seeds individually, 2.5 cm (1 in) deep in 7.5 cm (3 in) wide peat pots containing peat-based mixture, between mid- and late spring. The pots must be kept in either a greenhouse or indoors on a kitchen windowsill until the risk of frost has passed in late spring or early summer.

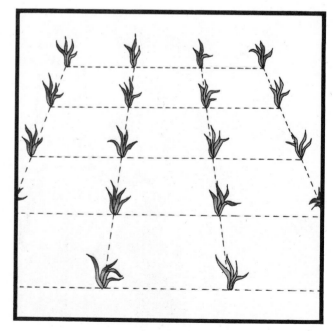

(2) Sweetcorn plants should be set out 45 cm (18 in) apart in rows 45 cm (18 in) apart. Since sweetcorn is pollinated by the wind, it is vital that you have a block of plants consisting of at least four rows, to provide satisfactory conditions for complete pollination.

Soil: Light, sandy and alkaline is the ideal, but heavy soil can be made suitable by the addition of plenty of compost; good drainage is vital.

Even with a small garden it is worth finding room for a row or two of this most delicious, luxury vegetable. Asparagus is not difficult to grow, as many people wrongly imagine, but you do need to be patient since it takes around three years for the plants to become fully productive. An asparagus bed has a useful life, however, of about 20 years.

Planting

Make a soil test to check on the alkalinity of the soil. In late autumn, cover the soil to a depth of 15 cm (6 in) with well-rotted garden compost or manure and dig or fork this into the soil. In late winter, add lime as necessary according to your soil test. The soil should ideally be pH 7.5. Order two-year old asparagus plants, called 'crowns', for delivery in mid-spring. These should be set in rows 38 cm (15 in) apart with 60 cm (2 ft) between the rows. Keep the bed free from weeds and make sure the plants do not go short of water. In early or midsummer give the bed an annual top dressing of vegetable fertilizer at the rate of 70 gm per sq m.

Pests and diseases

Asparagus beetles' larvae feed on the foliage and leave the stems bare. The remedy is to spray

(3) To make sure that the plants are properly pollinated, it is a good idea to give each plant a good shake once the flowers are fully formed to dislodge a shower of pollen from the top on to the female flowers below.

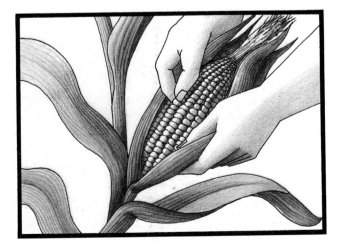

(4) The first sign that the cobs are ripening is

when the silks at the tops of the green-sheathed cobs turn brown. The next step is to make the thumbnail test. Pull back part of the sheath and squeeze a couple of corn grains between finger and thumbnail. If the liquid exuded is watery, the cob is not yet ripe. If the liquid is creamy, then you have cobs perfect for harvesting. If the liquid is 'doughy', then you are too late and the cobs are not fit for eating.

ASPARAGUS

(1) Prepare trenches for the plants, 15 cm (6 in) deep and 60 cm (2 ft) apart. At the foot of each trench, draw the soil into a slight ridge.

125

with derris if you see any greyish grubs. Cut worms eat young roots. Slugs eat shoots.

Harvesting
Do not cut any asparagus the first season after planting. In the second season, cut no more than one thick shoot from each plant. In the third season, cut all the shoots which appear in the first five weeks. In the fourth and the following seasons, cut all the shoots that appear up to mid early-summer. Then allow the bed to develop ferns. Store your surplus crop by freezing.

SPINACH

SPINACH
Sowing to harvest time: 8 to 15 weeks.
Yield: 230 gm (8 oz) to a plant.
Aspect: Shaded for summer varieties; open but sheltered for winter varieties.
Climate preferred: Cool temperate.
Soil type: Deep, moist and fertile.

Spinach can be tricky to produce on account of its natural tendency to run to seed instead of

(2) Place the plants in the trenches, with their roots well spread out, so that they are 38 cm (15 in) apart. The centre of the crown should rest on the ridge at the foot of the trench with roots sloping gently away.

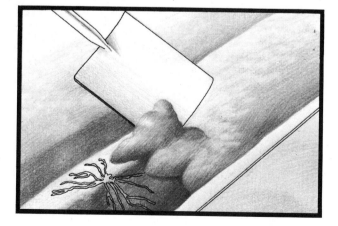

(3) Cover the plants with 7.5 cm to 10 cm (3 in to 4 in) of fine soil, leaving the rest of the soil to be washed into the trenches by the rain over the summer and autumn. Remove any large stones from around the trenches.

(4) As the ferns develop, provide them with a cage of bamboo canes and twine around the row for support. This is very important as, by encouraging the growth of the ferns, you will build up the strength of the plants and increase the following year's crop.

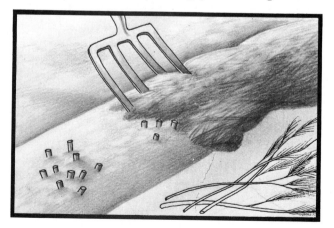

(5) In autumn, once the foliage has turned yellow, cut down the ferns to ground level and top dress the bed with well-rotted compost or manure.

producing lots of leaves. However, there are steps you can take to ensure success.

Sowing

The soil for spinach should contain plenty of organic matter and be limed if necessary. Two weeks before sowing, give the soil a top dressing of vegetable fertilizer at the rate of 135 gm per sq m (4 oz per sq yd). Summer spinach is best grown in the light shade of taller vegetables, for example as a catch crop between rows of peas and beans. Sow the seeds every few weeks from early spring to midsummer in rows 2.5 cm (1 in) deep and 30 cm (12 in apart). Thin the seedlings first to 7.5 cm (3 in) apart and some weeks later to 15 cm (6 in) apart. The plants from the second thinning will provide useful leaves for eating.

Winter spinach should be sown in late summer or early autumn (in warm districts) for harvesting between mid-autumn and mid-spring. In cold districts cover the crop with cloches in late autumn to protect it from frost. Hoe the soil around the plants regularly to keep down weeds and to keep the soil surface open and crumbly. Plenty of water is

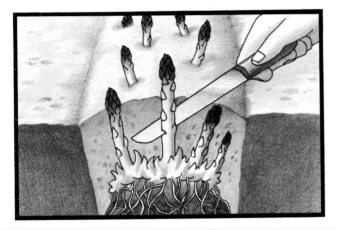

(6) To harvest asparagus, make a cut with a knife 2.5 cm (1 in) below soil level when the shoots are 10 cm (4 in) high. A saw-bladed knife, such as a bread knife, is ideal for this job as it cuts more cleanly.

SPINACH

(1) Summer spinach should ideally be sown in the shade of other taller vegetables such as peas and beans. Make the drills 2.5 cm (1 in) deep and sow the seeds as thinly as possible to avoid having to do a lot of unnecessary thinning out later.

In cold districts winter spinach should be covered with cloches in late autumn to protect it from snow and frost. If seakale beet is similarly covered during the winter, there will be a fresh crop of leaves for the following spring, summer and autumn. Otherwise you will have to sow a new crop in mid-spring.

(2) Leaf spinach should be harvested with scissors as soon as the leaves have reached an acceptable size. Continual cutting will encourage fresh growth. With summer varieties up to half the leaves can be removed at a time. With winter varieties, remove only a quarter of the leaves at a picking.

essential during dry spells.

Pests and diseases
Aphids and damping off.

Harvesting
Cut away the outer leaves when they reach an acceptable size. Store by freezing.

NEW ZEALAND SPINACH
Sowing to harvest time: 8 to 10 weeks.
Yield: 1 kg (2 lb) to a plant, but the more you pick the more you get.
Climate preferred: Cool temperate to subtropical.
Aspect: Sheltered.
Soil: Deep, moist and fertile.

New Zealand Spinach is not really a spinach, but it is an excellent and acceptable substitute in areas where the summers are often too dry for successful spinach growing.

Sowing
The soil should be prepared as for ordinary spinach. In mid late-spring the seeds should be soaked in water overnight to soften them and so speed germination. They should then be sown in clusters of three 1.3 cm ($\frac{1}{2}$ in) deep with 60 cm (2 ft) between subsequent clusters and other rows. Later thin out to leave just one plant 60 cm (2 ft) apart. Hoe to keep down weeds and water as necessary; although the plants tolerate drought, the leaves are much more succulent if they receive plenty of moisture. When the plants measure 30 cm (1 ft) across, remove their central growing points to encourage the formation of young leaves.

Pests and diseases
None of any consequence.

Harvesting
Cut a few leaves regularly from each plant to encourage the continued production of fresh young leaves.

SPINACH BEET
(also called perpetual spinach)
Sowing to harvest time: 8 to 14 weeks.
Yield: $\frac{1}{2}$ kg (1 lb) to a plant, but the more you cut the more you are likely to get.
Climate preferred: Cool temperate to subtropical.

(3) New Zealand spinach seeds should be soaked overnight before sowing to speed germination. Then the seeds should be placed in clusters of three in rows 1.3 cm ($\frac{1}{2}$ in) deep with 60 cm (2 ft) between subsequent clusters and rows. Thin out later to leave just one plant 60 cm (2 ft) apart.

(4) The stems of seakale beet should be grasped low down and pulled like rhubarb. They should not be cut, since cutting makes them bleed. Harvest the stems from the outsides of the plants first to enable the central stems to develop.

128

Aspect: Open or slightly shaded.
Soil: Ordinary, including poor and sandy soil.

Spinach beet is the easiest form of spinach to grow. It does not run to seed in summer or die of cold in winter. Its mild taste is often much preferred to that of ordinary spinach.

Sowing
The soil should be prepared as for ordinary spinach. In spring sow the seeds 2.5 cm (1 in) deep in drills 45 cm (18 in) apart. Later thin the seedlings to 20 cm (8 in) apart. The soil should be kept clear of weeds and the plants should be well watered when necessary.

Pests and diseases
None of any consequence.

Harvesting
The first leaves can be removed from the outside of the plants in summer, but the main point of spinach beet is to have spinach in winter and spring when the ordinary kind is scarce.

SILVER or SEAKALE BEET
(Swiss chard)
Sowing to harvest time: 12 weeks.
Yield: 1½ kg (3 lb) to a plant.
Climate preferred: Cool temperate to subtropical.
Aspect: Sun or shade.
Soil: Ordinary, including light sandy soil and heavy clay.

Seakale beet is easy to grow and it provides a continuous supply of spinach-like leaves throughout the summer and autumn. The leaves are cooked like ordinary spinach and the mid-ribs like asparagus. Alternatively both can be cooked together.

Sowing
The soil should be prepared as for ordinary spinach. In mid-spring sow three seeds together 1.3 cm (½ in) deep every 38 cm (15 in) in drills 45 cm (18 in) apart. As soon as the seedlings can be handled easily, thin to leave the strongest one every 38 cm (15 in) apart. The general cultivation of the crop is the same as for spinach.

Pests and diseases
None of any consequence.

Harvesting
It is essential to remove the stems from the outsides of the plants as if you were pulling rhubarb.

VEGETABLE FRUITS

AUBERGINE
(eggplant)
Sowing to harvest time: 22 to 26 weeks.
Yield: Four fruits to a plant.
Climate preferred: Subtropical.
Aspect: Sunny and sheltered.
Soil: Rich and fertile or potting mixture in a pot or growing bag.

With the introduction of hybrid aubergines, the growing of this particular vegetable has become much simpler and less dependent on the vagaries of the climate.

Sowing and planting
Aubergine seeds should be sown in late winter or early spring and the plants kept indoors in a sunny position where the temperature is as near to 21 C (70 F) as possible. Each plant is best restricted to producing just four fruits to ensure proper ripening.

Pests and diseases
Generally trouble free.

Harvesting
Cut the aubergines from the plants from late midsummer onwards while the bloom is still on their skins. As the shine disappears the fruit tends to become bitter. Store by freezing.

PEPPERS
Capsicum, sweet pepper, green pepper and red pepper
Sowing to harvest time: 20 to 26 weeks.
Yield: Varies according to the variety, but generally 680 to 960 gm (1½ to 2 lb) to a plant.
Climate preferred: Subtropical.
Aspect: Sunny and sheltered.
Soil: Rich and fertile, or potting mixture in a pot or growing bag.

Capsicums come in all shapes and sizes. A red pepper is simply a green pepper which has been left out in the sun.

Sowing and planting

Capsicum seeds should be sown in early or mid-spring and the plants kept indoors in a sunny position where the temperature is as close to 18°C (65°F) as possible. The general cultivation is the same as that for aubergines.

Pests and diseases

Aphids.

Harvesting

Begin to pick the fruits when they are still green—unless you want some red peppers. Store by freezing.

CUCUMBER
(indoor and outdoor)

Sowing to harvest time: 10 to 12 weeks indoors; 12 to 14 weeks outdoors.
Yield: 25 fruits to a plant.
Climate preferred: Subtropical.
Aspect: Sunny and sheltered.
Soil: Well-drained and rich in organic matter outdoors; potting mixture in growing bags indoors.

Cucumbers come in two basic types: the greenhouse cucumber with its beautiful long green fruits and the rather knobbly ridge cucumber which can be grown outdoors. The word 'ridge', incidentally, refers to the markings on the cucumber, not to the method of cultivation. Ridge cucumbers include gherkins for pickling.

Sowing and planting

Varieties for heated greenhouses, minimum night temperature 15°C (60°F), can be sown in late winter. The superior all-female varieties need a minimum night temperature of 21°C (70°F) and are beyond the pocket of most average gardeners because of the cost of fuel. For unheated greenhouses, cold frames and outdoors, sow two seeds 1.3 cm (½ in) deep in mid-spring in 7.5 cm (3 in) peat pots containing peat-based potting mixture. By placing the seeds on edge you will ensure better germination. If the pots are stood in a dark spot where the temperature is above 18°C (65°F), the seedlings will appear in four to nine days. At this stage the plants should be stood on a warm, sunny windowsill. Once the plants have

---

AUBERGINE and PEPPERS

(1) **Sow three seeds of your chosen variety of aubergine or capsicum in each 7.5 cm (3 in) peat pot containing peat-based mixture. The seeds should be 1.3 cm (½ in) deep. Place the pots in a dark spot where the temperature is above 21°C (70°F) until the seeds germinate. Then move the pots to a sunny windowsill.**

As soon as the seedlings can be handled easily, thin to leave just one plant in each pot.

(2) **When the plants are 12.5 cm (5 in) tall, pinch out their tops to encourage them to become bushy. If the plants become too large for their peat pots, they can be planted in 12.5 cm (5 in) plastic pots containing peat-based mixture. In late spring the plants can be set out in the greenhouse, either four to a growing bag or singly in 38 cm (9 in) plastic pots containing peat-based mixture.**

developed their first true cucumber leaves, in addition to their oval seedling leaves, thin out to leave the strongest plant in each pot. Greenhouse cucumbers can be put in an unheated greenhouse in mid late-spring. The potting mixture should be kept moist, but not soaking, and the plants should be fed with a liquid general fertilizer every two weeks after the first fruits start to swell.

Outdoor cucumbers can be grown in growing bags filled with special mixture or 60 cm (2 ft) apart in specially prepared soil. Growing bags are the best choice for cucumbers in frames. Feed every two weeks with liquid fertilizer once the first fruits have formed.

Pests and diseases
Capsids (tattered holes in leaves—spray with derris), red spider (leaves marked with pale patches—spray with derris), slugs (protect plants with slug pellets) and botrytis.

Harvesting
Cut the fruits regularly once they are well developed to encourage further fruits to form.

MARROW, COURGETTE, PUMPKIN and SQUASH
Sowing to harvest time: 10 to 14 weeks.
Yield: Varies enormously according to the type—6 kg (13 lb) courgettes to a 3 m (10 ft) row; marrows and squashes yield at least 2 kg (4½ lb) to a plant; and pumpkins yield three to five fruits to a plant, weighing 9 to 14 kg (20 to 30 lb) each.
Climate preferred: Subtropical.
Aspect: Sheltered and sunny.
Soil: Well-drained and rich in organic matter.

Marrows can be obtained in bush and trailing varieties, yielding fruit which can be oval, sausage-shaped or almost round. Courgettes are special varieties of marrow which produce lots of small fruits over a long period. Squashes, or custard marrows, are a popular American vegetable, and produce fruit which is roundish and varies from 7.5 cm (3 in) to 25 cm (10 in) in diameter. Pumpkins and thick-skinned winter squashes store well.

Sowing and planting
The soil should be prepared outdoors in the same

(3) If you wish to plant in the garden, you should wait until early summer and set the plants 60 cm (2 ft) apart. The soil for aubergines and peppers outdoors should be prepared by forking in plenty of compost and top dressing with vegetable fertilizer at the rate of 135 gm per sq m (4 oz per sq yd).

(4) Whether the plants are growing out of doors or in the greenhouse, they should be provided with bamboo canes for support.

131

way as for outdoor cucumbers. Bush types can be grown 60 cm (2 ft) apart each way, while trailing types should be at least 1.2 m (4 ft) apart each way. When the risk of frost has passed, generally in late spring, sow three seeds 2.5 cm (1 in) deep at each planting position. Put down slug pellets as a safety measure. As soon as the seedlings have two rough leaves, in addition to their seedling leaves, thin to leave just one plant at each position. The soil should be kept moist at all times. The tips of the main shoots of trailing types should be pinched

off when they reach 90 cm (3 ft) long. Once the fruits start to swell, feed with a liquid general fertilizer every two weeks. Weeds are best prevented rather than removed by putting down a 2.5 cm (1 in) layer of moist peat around the plants. In cold districts plants can be covered with cloches or grown in cold frames or cold greenhouses.

Pests and diseases
Capsids (tattered holes in leaves—spray with derris), red spider (leaves marked with pale

(5) Once the flowers appear, spray gently with lukewarm water to encourage fruit to form. The plants should also be fed every two weeks with a liquid general fertilizer.

CUCUMBERS and MARROWS

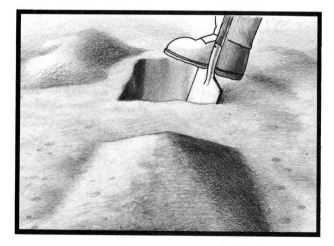

(1) Cucumbers and members of the marrow tribe should be grown outdoors in specially prepared pockets of soil. Take out holes for the plants the width and depth of your spade. Then fill the holes with an equal mixture of

well-rotted compost (or manure) and soil so that you end up with a 7.5 cm (3 in) high mound at each planting position. Finally top dress the soil around the planting positions with vegetable fertilizer at the rate of 135 gm per sq m (4 oz per sq yd).

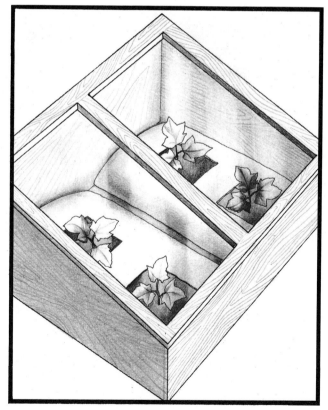

(2) Cucumbers and members of the marrow tribe can also be grown in specially prepared growing bags. You will be able to get two plants in each bag. Such bags are the best method of growing in cold frames. In cold districts the plants can be covered with cloches which are at least 38 cm (15 in) wide.

patches—spray with derris), slugs and botrytis.

Harvesting

Cut courgettes when they are 10 cm (4 in) long; marrows are best when 25 cm (10 in) long. Constant cutting is essential to prolong fruiting. Marrows, pumpkins and squashes required for winter storage should be allowed to mature on the plants and should be cut before the first frosts are expected. Store on slatted shelves or in plastic nets in a cool, frost-free shed or garage.

TOMATO

Sowing to harvest time: greenhouse varieties, 18 weeks; outdoor varieties, 20 weeks.

Yield: 4 to 5 kg (9 to 11 lb) to a plant indoors; 2 kg (2½ lb) to a plant outdoors.

Climate preferred: Subtropical. Tomatoes cannot stand frost.

Aspect: Sunny

Soil: Potting mixture gives best results indoors; outdoors the plants need rich, moisture-retentive soil, or you can use growing bags.

(3) **Outdoor cucumbers should have their growing tops removed when they have produced seven leaves. Side-shoots will then develop and these can be pinched out at four leaves. Once the fruit has formed, the fruiting side-shoots should have their tops removed at a point two leaves beyond the tiny cucumber.**

(5) **In late spring, greenhouse cucumbers should be set in growing bags or in 23 cm (9 in) wide plastic pots containing peat-based mixture.**

(4) **Once the first fruits have formed, support them on pieces of wood or tile to keep them clean and free from the attentions of slugs. Bush marrows, or bush courgettes, will need support from several bamboo canes once they are 90 cm (3 ft) high.**

(6) **The main shoot should be allowed to grow until it reaches the desired height, when the top can be pinched off. Canes and wires on the greenhouse wall should be provided for support.**

Left: A heavy crop of tomatoes.

Tomatoes are not at all difficult to grow if you choose the most suitable varieties for your intended purpose and location. Outdoors, bush varieties are the best choice in cold districts. They can also be covered with cloches to speed the ripening of the fruit.

Sowing and planting

If you can provide heat in your greenhouse to raise the temperature to 10°C (50°F) by night, seed can be sown in early winter to raise plants for setting out in early spring. However, if the greenhouse is unheated, the seed should not be sown until mid early-spring to produce plants for setting out later in mid- or late spring for a midsummer crop. The seed to produce plants for outdoor growing should be sown in early mid-spring. The alternative is to buy plants from a nursery when you require them.

Pests and diseases

Aphids, white fly (spray the undersides of the leaves with malathion and repeat at seven-day intervals), blight (leaves and fruit turn brown—spray with Bordeaux powder from early midsummer) and damping off (seedlings).

Harvesting

Gather the fruit when it is well-coloured. Greenhouse tomatoes can be left on the plants to the first frosts. Outdoor fruit is best picked by early autumn and the remaining green fruit allowed to ripen on a windowsill. Store the surplus crop by freezing.

(7) Train the side-shoots along the wires and pinch off their tops at the second leaf joint, beyond a female flower.

(8) With greenhouse cucumber varieties all male flowers should be removed as fertilized fruit is bitter. Female flowers can be dis- tinguished by the miniature cucumber behind their petals. This procedure does **NOT** apply to ridge cucumbers.

TOMATOES

(1) Sow the seed very thinly in a seed tray containing a suitable compost and germinate them in a dark spot where the temperature is around 18°C (65°F). Once the seedlings appear in a week or so, move the seed tray into the light. As soon as the seedlings are large enough to handle, move them to 7.5 cm (3 in) peat pots containing peat-based mixture and

HERBS

As any good cook will soon tell you, even with all these vegetables in our gardens, there are some vital ingredients missing—herbs. These plants and shrubs take up little space and are invaluable in the kitchen for flavouring food. There is room in every garden to grow a few herbs—they are happy to grow among the vegetables, fruit and flowers. However,

if you do have enough space, then a special herb garden will also provide you with a colourful and sweet-smelling array of plants that more than compensate for the small amount of time and effort involved in growing them.

Here are six herbs which are suited to most gardens and will be most welcome to any cook. Remember that herb leaves for drying should be harvested on a dry day before any flowers are

keep the pots on a sunny windowsill until the plants can be set out in their final positions.

(2) The soil for tomatoes outdoors should be prepared by digging in plenty of compost and top dressing with vegetable fertilizer at the rate of 135 gm per sq m (4 oz per sq yd). Tomato plants should be set 60 cm (2 ft) apart outdoors and the plants provided with stout bamboo canes or wooden stakes for support. Train the plants to their supports as they increase in height.

house or outdoors, remove the side-shoots which form at the point where the leaves meet the main stem to restrict the plants to this one main stem. This does NOT apply to bush varieties which need no such attention. However, in cold districts bush varieties may need to be covered with cloches.

(4) When the plants being grown outdoors with a single stem have produced four trusses (bunches) of fruit, remove the tops to stop further growth and to help the fruit ripen.

(3) As the plants grow, whether in a green-

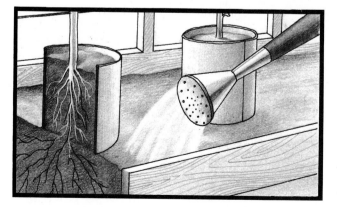

(5) It is not a good idea to grow tomatoes in the greenhouse soil as this leads to disease.

136

fully out.

CHIVES
Hardy perennial
Spread: 20 by 30 cm (8 by 12 in)
Position: Sun or light shade.
Soil: Any, provided that it is well-drained.
Sowing: Sow in early or mid-spring in rows 1 cm (½ in) deep. Thin the seedlings to 15 cm (6 in) apart.

Seed can also be sown indoors and one seedling placed in each 12.5 cm (5 in) pot. The leaves can be used for months after sowing.

Harvesting: Cut the leaves close to the ground to encourage further growth. Remove any pink flowers which appear.

Storing: Leaves may be frozen for use in winter.

Far better to use tomato growing bags or to plant your tomato plants in 23 cm (9 in) wide bottomless ring pots, filled with potting mixture and standing on a 15 cm (6 in) thick base of gravel, cinders or coarse sand. This latter method of tomato growing is called 'ring culture'. Initially the soil in the rings is watered, but once the roots have reached the aggregate at the bottom, water is applied only to the gravel or sand, while tomato fertilizer is applied to the pot. This method of growing can result in huge crops.

(7) Water tomato plants frequently and start to feed once a week with tomato fertilizer once the first truss of fruit has formed.

HERBS

(1) Most shrub herbs can be raised inexpensively and easily by seed sowing outdoors. Both rosemary and sage can be sown in a small nursery bed in a warm, sheltered spot, and the plants later transferred to their final positions.

(6) Tomatoes in a greenhouse can be provided with canes for support. An easier method of supporting the plants is to suspend strings from the glazing bars on the greenhouse roof and to wind the plants around the strings as they grow upwards.

137

MINT
Hardy perennial
Spread: 30 by 45 cm plus (12 by 18 in plus).
Position: Sun or partial shade.
Soil: Moist and fertile.
Planting: In spring or autumn plant pieces of root in 25 or 30 cm (10 or 12 in) clay pots containing good soil or a proprietary potting mixture and sink the pots in the garden soil so that the rims are level with the soil surface.

Harvesting: Gather the leaves as required.

Storing: Freezing or drying.

ROSEMARY
Hardy evergreen shrub.
Spread: 60 cm to 1.5 m by 60 cm to 1.5 m (2 to 5 ft by 2 to 5 ft).
Position: Sunny and sheltered.
Soil: Light and well-drained.

Sowing and planting: Sow seeds in early spring outdoors 6 mm ($\frac{1}{4}$ in) deep. Thin as required and transplant to a final spacing of 60 cm (2 ft) apart. Or buy shrubs in spring from a nursery.

Harvesting: Cut sprigs as required.

Storing: Unnecessary as rosemary is evergreen.

SAGE
Shrubs with a useful life of three years.
Spread: 30 to 60 cm by 45 cm (1 to 2 ft by 18 in).
Position: Warm and sunny.
Soil: Any, provided that it is well-drained.
Sowing and planting: Sow the seeds 6 mm ($\frac{1}{4}$ in) deep in a nursery bed in early summer, thin and move the plants to their final positions the following spring 60 cm (2 ft) apart. Alternatively, shrubs from a nursery can be set out in spring.

Harvesting: Gather leaves as required.

Storing: Leaves for drying should be picked in late spring.

Right: A larger-than-average herb garden.

(2) **Before sowing parsley, soak the seed overnight in a saucer of warm water. This speeds up the germination process and ensures success.**

(3) **If mint is planted in the garden soil, it soon spreads rapidly by means of its invasive underground roots and becomes a nuisance. For this reason it is best planted in a 25 cm or 30 cm (10 in or 12 in) clay pot containing good soil and the pot sunk in the garden soil so that its rim is level with the soil surface. The point in using a clay pot instead of a plastic one is that clay allows the two-way passage of moisture.**

PARSLEY

Biennial, but best treated as an annual.
Spread: 25 by 25 cm (10 by 10 in).
Position: Sunny and sheltered.
Soil: Rich and moist.
Sowing: Sow in early or mid-spring for summer and autumn harvest; sow in midsummer for winter and spring. Sow the seed as thinly as possible in drills no more than 6 mm ($\frac{1}{4}$ in) deep. Germination takes three to six weeks. Thin the seedlings to 23 cm (9 in) apart. Seedlings can also be planted in 12.5 cm (5 in) diameter pots containing a suitable potting mixture. Remove flowers if they appear.

Harvesting: Cut as required.

Storing: Freezing or drying.

THYME

Shrub/herbacious perennial with a useful life of three years.
Spread: 23 by 23 cm (9 by 9 in).
Position: Full sun.
Soil: Any, provided that it is well-drained.
Planting: Nursery-grown stock should be set out 23 cm (9 in) apart in early or mid-spring. Alternatively each plant can be accommodated in a 15 cm (6 in) diameter pot containing a proprietary potting mixture. After three years, the plants can be lifted in spring, divided and replanted.

Harvesting: Pick the leaves as required.

Storing: Dry leaves picked before the flowers appear in early summer.

(4) After three years, thyme plants begin to deteriorate and the branches become straggly. At this point it is best to lift the plants in spring and to divide them into smaller pieces. The best of these small pieces can be replanted. The remainder of the plant is best discarded.

(5) Herb leaves for drying should be harvested on a dry day before any flowers are fully out. Wash the leaves carefully under a running tap. Then tie smaller leaved herbs in small bundles and hang them up to dry. Larger leaved herbs, such as mint, should have the leaves stripped from the stems and laid out on a wire cake tray to dry. Once the leaves are dried, they can be crushed with a rolling pin before being placed in airtight glass storage jars.

Fruits

If you are going to plant a tree in your back garden, why not make it one which bears fruit? The blossom in spring of the apple, apricot, peach or pear is every bit as eye-catching as any other flowering tree or shrub. But best of all there is the delight of being able to pick one's own fruit... whether it be a tree fruit, or a soft fruit such as strawberry, or a fruit such as grape or rhubarb which does not belong in either category.

autumn and early spring during a spell when the weather is mild and the soil is workable. Container-grown trees from nurseries or garden shops can be planted at any time, provided they are watered regularly after planting. With all fruit trees, it is wise to follow an annual spraying programme to eliminate pests and diseases and to ensure perfect crops of fruit. Refer to the individual fruits for the treatment required.

The soft fruits—blueberries, currants, gooseberries, raspberries, strawberries and others—are an excellent choice, particularly if yours is a smaller than average garden. Soft fruits can, if necessary, be accommodated among other shrubs and plants.

Strawberries can be grown in tubs on a patio, while a grape vine or loganberry makes a handsome and useful addition to a house wall. Certain bush fruits, such as the blueberry which is very fussy about its soil and the fig which requires some restriction on its roots, are also a good choice for growing in containers.

The 'yield' suggested for each fruit is the amount that may be achieved on average each year.

TREE FRUITS

APPLE
Type of tree: Bush, standard, half-standard, cordon and espalier.
Pollination: At least two trees are necessary to produce fruit.
Climate preferred: Temperate.
Aspect: Any. Early cooking apples can be grown against north-facing walls.
Ideal Soil: Well-drained ordinary soil which does not dry out excessively in summer.
Yield: 10 cordons will produce 20 kg (44 lb) of fruit; the same harvest can be obtained from one standard or half-standard, four bush trees or four espaliers.

Planting and cultivation
The soil for apples can be made suitable by the addition of plenty of compost. For the first few years put down a moisture-retaining layer of compost or moist peat around the trees' roots in mid-spring and water thoroughly during dry spells. Every early spring top dress the soil around the spread of the branches with general fertilizer at the rate of 35 gm per sq m (4 oz per sq yd). In early

There are fruit trees of all shapes and sizes to suit most gardens. It is just a matter of choosing a form of tree to fit in with your garden, no matter how small it may be.

Pollination of fruit trees is normally carried out by insects. Some trees are described as self-fertile because fruit is produced through insects transferring pollen from one flower to another on the same tree. Apricots, peaches, nectarines, some plums and all soft fruits are self-fertile. Other fruit trees require the pollen of the same type, but from different varieties to ensure that the flowers develop into fruit. Before buying fruit trees, find out first from the nursery what are the most suitable and compatible trees for your area.

The normal time for planting is between late

summer many of the smaller apples will be shed naturally from the tree. If the tree still appears to be bearing too heavy a crop, thin out the remainder and remove any inferior apples by cutting them from the tree with secateurs. If you allow a tree to produce too many apples one year, it will in all probability yield no fruit at all the following year.

Harvesting

An apple is ready for picking if, when you cradle it in your hand and twist it gently, it comes away easily from the tree. Store the surplus crop which cannot be eaten within a few weeks either by freezing, or by wrapping the individual apples in newspaper and storing them in ventilated boxes or on racks in a cool humid place.

Pests and diseases

Aphids, capsids, codling moth (grubs tunnel into fruit), sawfly, mildew and scab.

The best plan is to have an annual spraying plan to give complete protection. Spray in winter with a tar oil wash. At bud burst, spray with an insecticide and a systemic fungicide. Spray again with insecticide and systemic fungicide at the green bud stage as the first leaves unfold; again at the pink bud stage; again at petal fall; and again at the fruitlet stage; and repeat three weeks after the fruitlet stage using only insecticide to give full protection against the grubs of the codling moth.

Pruning

Standard, half-standard and bush trees can be

(1) Bush trees are the most popular form of tree for modern small gardens and they enable a considerable quantity of fruit to be grown. They have a trunk which is about 60 cm (2 ft) high and they average 2.5 to 3 m (8 to 10 ft) in height with a 3 to 3.5 m (10 to 12 ft) spread. Fruits usually grown in bush form include apples, pears, peaches, nectarines, plums, gages, damsons and cherries. They are normally planted at least 3.5 m (12 ft) apart.

(2) Cordon trees might almost have been developed specially for today's small gardens since no other form of tree enables so much fruit to be grown in a restricted space. A cordon has a single stem with very short side branches and it can either be trained at an angle of 45° against wires in the open, or upright against a house wall. Cordons grow to 3 m (10 ft) in length with a 45 cm (18 in) spread and are planted in rows with 60 to 90 cm (2 to 3 ft) between the individual trees, although they could be planted much farther apart if you wish. Apples and pears are usually the only ones grown in this form.

143

pruned, only if necessary, in winter. It is a mistake to prune apple trees more than is absolutely essential as it often stimulates unwanted growth. Cordon trees are pruned in autumn. Espalier trees are pruned in autumn and winter.

PEAR

Type of tree: Bush, standard, half-standard, cordon and espalier.
Pollination: At least two trees are required to produce fruit.
Climate preferred: Temperate.
Aspect: Sunny, or facing south or west, and sheltered from strong winds.
Ideal Soil: Well-drained deep soil which does not dry out excessively in summer.
Yield: 10 cordons will produce 20 kg (44 lb) of fruit; a similar harvest can be obtained from one standard, or half-standard, four bush trees or four espaliers.

Planting and cultivation
Success with pears depends largely on your choosing the best possible varieties for your district. The world famous 'Conference' and 'William's Bon Chrétien' are the best choice for cold, higher altitude areas or exposed coastal districts. The soil should be improved by the addition of plenty of compost. Every early spring feed the soil around the spread of the branches with general fertilizer at the rate of 135 gm per sq m (4 oz per sq yd). In mid-spring surround the trees with a thick moisture-retaining layer of compost or moist peat. Pears are less tolerant of dry soil conditions than apples, and if the soil in early summer is not sufficiently moist, the normal early summer drop of immature fruitlets can turn into a shedding of the entire crop.

Harvesting
Pears should not be allowed to become completely

(3) Espalier, or horizontal branched trees, have a single central stem and two or three pairs of branches on either side which are trained on wires, either fixed to posts in the open or to a suitable wall. Apples and pears are the only tree fruits grown by this method. The trees grow to 1.8 to 2.4 m (6 to 8 ft) tall, depending on how many 'tiers' of branches are chosen and they are planted 3.6 m (12 ft) apart.

(4) Fan-shaped trees have short trunks and their branches are trained on wires on a wall, or fence, in the form of the ribs of a lady's fan. This type of training is normally reserved for the more exotic trees such as apricots, figs, peaches and nectarines, as well as cherries and plums. The height of the average fan tree on an outside wall is 3 m (10 ft) with a spread of 3 to 4.5 m (10 to 15 ft). If more than one tree is grown, they should be spaced 3.6 m (12 ft) apart.

144

ripe on the tree if they are to be eaten at their best. Early varieties (late summer, early autumn) should be cut from the tree while the fruit is still hard; mid-season varieties (mid- and late autumn) should be picked as soon as the fruit can be cupped in the hand and twisted gently free from the tree; late varieties (early winter onwards) can be harvested at the same stage of ripeness as mid-season pears. To store, the crop should be laid out in single layers on slatted shelves or in boxes in a cool shed or garage. The pears should not touch, nor should they be wrapped. Final ripening can be achieved by taking the fruit into a warm room for three days. If properly stored, pears will keep for months.

Pruning

Pears are pruned and trained in exactly the same way as apples. However, they can stand much more severe cutting back, and in summer the pruning of cordons and espaliers may have to begin several weeks earlier than the routine pruning of apples.

Pests and diseases

Aphids, birds and wasps (do not let the fruit remain too long on the trees), capsids and scab.

As with apples, it is best to have an annual spraying programme. Spray in winter with tar oil wash. Spray with insecticide at green bud stage (as leaves unfold), white bud stage and petal fall. Spray with systemic fungicide at leaf bud burst, as the first leaves unfold, at white bud, petal fall and fruitlet stages.

APRICOT
Type of tree: Bush (suitable only in warm, sheltered gardens) and fan-trained.
Pollination: Self-fertile.
Climate: Subtropical to temperate.
Aspect: Sunny or facing south or west.

(5) Standard or half-standard trees have the same shape as a bush, except that standards have 1.8 m (6 ft) trunks and a spread of 6 m (20 ft) and half-standards have 1.2 m (4 ft) trunks and a spread of 4.5 m (15 ft). Apples, pears, plums and sweet cherries are all grown in this form, which is difficult to manage successfully in an ordinary garden. However, if you fancy lazing on the lawn in the shade of an apple tree, then this is the tree for you. With standard and half-standard trees, subsequent trees should be spaced at least 6 m (20 ft) apart. If you have insufficient room for two such trees, the problem of pollination can be overcome by planting a smaller form of tree of the same type close by.

(6) The soil for fruit trees should be thoroughly broken up with a fork to a depth of 45 cm (18 in) and sufficient soil removed from the planting hole to accommodate the tree's roots comfortably. With bush and standard (as well as half-standard) a sturdy stake should be hammered into the hole to support the tree before it is actually planted.

145

Ideal Soil: Any provided that it is fertile and well-drained.

Yield: 50 to 60 fruits annually.

Planting and cultivation

The soil can be improved if necessary by adding compost, but avoid excessive use of fertilizers, particularly in the case of fan-trained trees, as too rich a soil encourages unnecessary leafy growth. The branches of fan trees should be secured loosely to a framework of wires. In cold districts you can also grow peaches by training a fan tree against wires on one of the walls inside a greenhouse with a span of at least 3 m (10 ft). No heat is necessary. In early spring top dress the soil around the trees with general fertilizer at the rate of 135 gm per sq m (4 oz per sq yd) under the spread of the branches. In mid-spring surround the trees with a thick layer of compost or moist peat. Although apricots are self-fertile, you will often do better to pollinate the tree yourself by dabbing the centre of each open flower in turn with an artist's brush. Thinning the fruit is rarely necessary, but when the fruitlets are 2.5 cm (1 in) wide, ensure that the crop is evenly spaced over the tree with 10 cm (4 in) between each fruit. Water the soil thoroughly whenever the weather is dry while the fruits are swelling to prevent them from splitting.

Harvesting

Pick apricots as soon as they are ripe and well coloured and can be pulled easily from the tree.

Pruning and training

Bush trees need no regular pruning other than the removal of dead, diseased, weak and crossing branches in spring. With fan trees, the best plan is to invest at the start in the best shaped tree you can get, since producing the ideal fan shape on a young tree is somewhat difficult for amateurs.

(7) **Trim off any damaged roots with your secateurs. Then plant the tree so that the nursery soil mark on the trunk is at the same level as your garden soil. Fill in around the roots with good garden soil or soil enriched by mixing it with some well-rotted compost or peat. Shake the tree from time to time to get the soil to settle around the roots and firm the soil around the trunk with your heel. Finally use a tree-tie or an old nylon stocking, looped in a figure eight, to secure the trunk to the stake. If the tree is growing in a grassed area, it is essential to keep a bare weed-free circle of soil at least 1 m (3 ft) around its trunk for several years to enable**

it to become established without competition from the grass for moisture and plant foods.

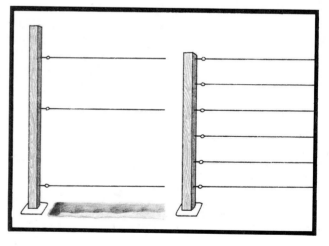

(8) **Cordon and espalier trees should have their supporting framework of wires set up before you get around to planting. For a row of cordons stretch wires between sturdy hardwood posts (or concrete or metal posts) at 30 cm (1 ft), 1.5 m (5 ft) and 2 m (7 ft) from the ground. It is vital that the supporting posts should be set into concrete and that the wires are held taut by means of tension bolts. For espalier trees stretch wires every 30 cm (1 ft) to a height of 1.5 to 1.8 m (5 to 6 ft), depending on the number of 'tiers'.**

146

However, assuming that you have a good tree, the side-shoots should be pinched back to 7.5 cm (3 in) in late spring and early summer and the secondary side-shoots (sub-laterals) to one leaf. Crossing and crowded branches should also be removed at this time. In autumn cut away those side-shoots which have borne fruit and tie in the replacement growths from the base of the side-shoots. If the 'ribs' of the fan grow beyond their allotted space in a greenhouse, cut them back to a strong side-shoot.

Pests and diseases

Aphids, birds and wasps (protect with fine netting or plastic mesh netting), red spider mites (greenhouse trees have a pale mottling on the leaves—spray with malathion).

PEACHES and NECTARINES
Type of tree: Bush or fan-trained.

Pollination: Self-fertile.
Climate preferred: Subtropical to temperate.
Aspect: Sunny, or facing south or west.
Ideal Soil: Any, provided that it is well-drained.
Yield: 50 to 60 fruits annually.

Planting and cultivation

Peaches are, despite their exotic appearance, no more difficult to grow in most parts than plums. Yet a home-grown peach is vastly superior to anything which you can buy from the shops; the fruit is large, very juicy and deliciously perfumed. A nectarine is simply a kind of peach with a smooth skin with none of the characteristic peach fuzz. Whereas peaches can be grown outdoors in fairly cold areas, nectarines are less hardy and are best with the additional protection of a sunny wall. Both peaches and nectarines are excellent fruits to grow in a greenhouse with a span of at least 3 m

The soil for cordons and espaliers should be prepared in the same way as for ordinary fruit trees. However, with cordons it may be found more convenient if prior to planting you take out a shallow trench the entire length of the row.

secured more easily to the wires and also take some of the strain off the graft between stem and rootstock.

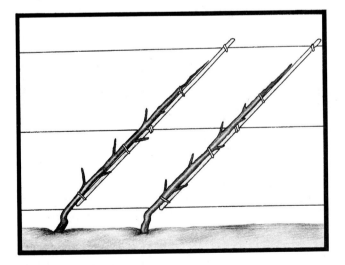

(9) Cordons are planted at an angle of 45° with the point where the tree was grafted uppermost. Ideally the stems of trees should point towards the north (or south in the southern hemisphere) to ensure that they get the maximum sunshine. Provide bamboo splints for the stems so that they can be

(10) Crowded and crossing branches, also diseased and damaged shoots, can be removed from standard, half-standard and bush apple and pear trees in winter. The idea is to produce an open-centred tree which looks like a goblet-shaped wine glass. However, be careful not to remove too many fruit-producing growths, which are the generally plump and rather rounded buds. Some varieties produce their fruit from buds on short growths known as spurs, while others

147

(10 ft). The trees should be planted in late autumn in soil which has been improved as necessary by the addition of well-rotted compost. The branches of fan trees should be lightly secured to a framework of wires. In early spring give the soil around the spread of the branches a top dressing of general fertilizer at the rate of 135 gm per sq m (4 oz per sq yd). Then in mid-spring put down a moisture-retaining and weed-suppressing layer of compost or moist peat.

Like all stone fruits, peaches and nectarines are shallow rooting. So cultivation of the soil near the trees must be kept to a minimum. Although the trees are self-fertile, it is best to pollinate them yourself by dabbing the centre of each flower in turn with an artist's brush. Peaches and nectarines, incidentally, will cross-pollinate each other, thus improving the chances of a good crop. Blossom and fruitlets can be protected from spring frosts with a double thickness of lightweight plastic netting. Plenty of water should be given whenever the soil dries out. Nectarines especially require regular watering while the fruits are swelling to prevent them from splitting. Thinning of the fruit is generally unnecessary, but if some are overcrowded, thin when the fruits are around 2.5 cm (1 in) in diameter and leave the remainder 23 cm (9 in) apart.

Harvesting
Pick peaches and nectarines when the flesh around the stalks yields to light pressure from the fingers. The surplus crop will keep for a month if stored in a cool place.

Pruning and training
Dead, damaged and crossing branches should be removed from bush trees in late spring. On established bushes, older branches can also be cut away when they become unfruitful. With fan trees,

---

have their fruit-producing buds mainly at the tips of the previous season's shoots. It is essential that you decide which are fruit buds and whether the tree is a spur or tip-bearer before you start wielding the secateurs.

bark colour. If the spurs on mature cordons become overcrowded, particularly on pears, thin out or remove completely in winter.

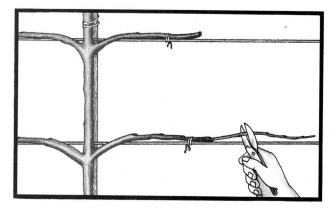

(11) With cordon trees, cut back the new growth on the side branches in early autumn to four leaves beyond the cluster of leaves on the original spur. In late autumn the length of the main stem of the cordon can be shortened by as much as a third. Shorten the new growth again on the side branches to within two or three buds of the base of the previous season's wood. Old wood can be distinguished from new wood by its darker

(12) The new growth from the spurs on the horizontal branches of espalier trees is pruned in autumn in exactly the same way as for cordons. The extension growth of the horizontal branches, by which the tree increases in width, should be cut back by up to half of its new growth in winter, depending on its vigour. Weak branches are always cut back more severely. Once the main side branches have reached the desired length, say 1.8 m (6 ft), they can be pruned annually in autumn as if they too were side-shoots arising from the fruiting spurs.

pinch back the side-shoots in late spring and early summer to the sixth leaf and the secondary side-shoots (sub-laterals) to one leaf. Crossing, crowded and dead branches should also be removed. In autumn, after picking the fruit, cut back each side-shoot which has borne fruit to its replacement, and secure the replacement shoots to the wires with twine. Once the extension growth from the 'ribs' of the fan reach their allotted space, treat them as if they too were fruit-bearing side-shoots. If gaps appear in the fan structure, either through disease or neglect, fill them by retaining some of the side-shoots which have borne fruit and tie these shoots to the wires.

Pests and diseases

Aphids, birds and wasps (protect with fine netting or plastic mesh netting), red spider mites (greenhouse trees have a pale mottling on their leaves—spray with malathion), leaf curl (leaves develop reddish blisters and drop from tree—spray with lime sulphur in autumn and just before the leaf buds swell and burst in spring).

PLUMS, GAGES and DAMSONS

Type of tree: Bush, half-standard and fan-trained (not damsons).

Pollination: All damsons, and some plums and gages are self-fertile. The remainder need the pollen from another variety flowering at the same time to produce a crop of fruit.

Climate preferred: Temperate.

Aspect: Sunny, or facing east or west. The 'Victoria' plum will produce a good crop even on a north-facing wall.

Ideal Soil: Well-drained loam or clay containing a little lime.

Yield: One tree will supply enough fruit for the average family.

(13) With fan-trained apricots, peaches and nectarines, pinch back the side-shoots in late spring and early summer to the sixth leaf and the secondary side-shoots (sub-laterals) to one leaf. Crossing, crowded and dead branches can also be removed at this time. In autumn, after picking the fruit, cut back each side-shoot which has borne fruit to its replacement, and secure the replacement shoots to the wires with raffia or twine. Once the extension growth from the 'ribs' of the fan reach their alloted space, treat them as if they too were fruit-bearing side-shoots. If gaps appear in the fan, either through disease or neglect, fill them by retaining some of the shoots which have borne fruit and tie these shoots to the wires.

(14) Remove dead, diseased, crowded and outward-growing shoots on fan plum, gage and cherry trees in spring. In midsummer all side-shoots which are not required should be pinched back to the sixth leaf. After the crop has been harvested, cut back by half all those shoots which were previously pinched back. If the extension growth of the fan grows beyond its allotted space, cut the branches back at this time to a strong side branch.

Planting and cultivation

The trees should be planted in well-prepared soil in late autumn or early winter. In early spring top dress the soil with general fertilizer at the rate of 135 gm per sq m (4 oz per sq yd) under the spread of the branches. In mid-spring put down a thick moisture-retaining and weed-suppressing layer of compost. Soil cultivation should be avoided to prevent damage to the trees' surface roots. Thin the crop in early summer if necessary to take the weight off any obviously overladen branches. Leave the remaining fruits about 5 cm (2 in) apart.

Harvesting

Pick the fruit carefully by the stalk to prevent bruising. Dessert plums and gages are best left on the tree until they are completely ripe; cooking plums and damsons should be gathered while they are still hard.

Pruning

Bush, standard and half-standard trees need little actual pruning apart from the routine removal of dead and crowded shoots. Young trees should be pruned in spring, while established trees are best pruned in summer to enable the pruning cuts to heal and so prevent disease. Fan trees should have outward-growing shoots removed in spring. In midsummer all side-shoots which are not required should be pinched back to the sixth leaf. After the crop has been harvested, cut back by half all those shoots which were previously pinched back.

Pests and diseases

Aphids, birds and wasps (protect the fruit on fan trees with fine netting or plastic mesh netting). Little or no blossom indicates bullfinches (cover trees if possible with mesh netting in late winter and early spring).

CHERRY
(sour or cooking type).

Type of tree: Bush or fan-trained.
Pollination: Self-fertile.
Climate preferred: Temperate.

(15) **Before planting a fan-trained tree close to a wall, it is essential to improve the soil by forking it over to a depth of 45 cm (18 in) and adding plenty of well-rotted compost. For fan trees the wires should be secured to the wall or fence by bolts called 'vine eyes' so that you have a framework of horizontal wires at 23 cm (9 in) intervals to a height of 2 m (7 ft). Plant the tree so that its trunk is about 23 cm (9 in) out from the wall or fence and ensure that the nursery soil mark on the trunk corresponds to the same soil level as in your garden. In order to achieve the**

150

ideal fan shape, it is often an advantage to use bamboo canes as splints for training.

The side-shoots should be tied loosely to the wires with either raffia or twine so that there is some free movement to prevent their being snapped by the wind.

(16) **Although apricots, peaches and nectarines are self fertile, they flower early in the year when there are few insects around to do the pollinating. So it is best to do the job**

Aspect: Any including north-facing.
Ideal Soil: Any, provided that it is well-drained.
Yield: One tree is sufficient for most families.

Planting and cultivation

There are two kinds of cherry: sweet or dessert cherries, and cooking cherries. Unhappily, sweet cherries, even in fan-trained form, make very large trees which are unsuitable for the majority of gardens. Another snag is that sweet cherries need the pollen of another cherry tree to produce a crop of fruit. If that were not problems enough, birds have a huge appetite for sweet cherries, and protecting the crop in the garden is difficult. So plant your chosen variety of cooking cherry in well-prepared soil between late autumn and early spring and maintain a 1 m (3 ft) wide circle of soil around its trunk for several years. In early spring top dress the soil under the spread of the branches with general fertilizer at the rate of 135 gm per sq m (4 oz per sq yd). In mid-spring surround the tree with a thick moisture-retaining and weed-suppressing layer of compost.

Harvesting

The ripe fruit should be cut from the tree with secateurs or scissors to avoid damage to the shoots which can in turn lead to disease.

Pruning

Bush cherry trees should be pruned once they have started to fruit by thinning out some of the shoots in the centre to allow in light and air. Dead, crowded and crossing branches should be cut away in spring. However, with cherries the less pruning you do the better.

Pests and diseases

Aphids (cherry blackfly—spray with insecticide immediately after flowering).

CANE FRUITS

RASPBERRY
(summer and autumn fruiting kinds)
Size: 1.2 m to 2.4 m by 45 cm (4 ft to 8 ft by 1½ ft),

---

yourself by dabbing the centre of each open flower in turn with an artist's brush. Fan trees in greenhouses are always best hand pollinated.

(17) In areas where frosts are likely, the blossom on apricots, peaches and nectarines can be protected by covering the trees with a double thickness of lightweight plastic netting. If the weather is severe, the netting can be left on the trees to protect the young fruitlets.

CANE FRUIT

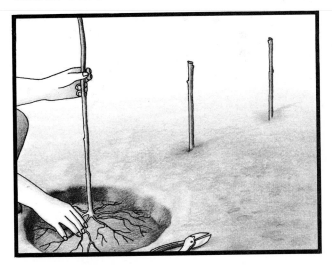

(1) Plant raspberries between late autumn and early spring when the weather is mild and the soil is not too wet. Plant so that the root system is about 7.5 cm (3 in) deep and the individual canes are about 45 cm (18 in) apart. Subsequent rows of raspberries should be at least 1.2 m (4 ft) apart. Cut back the canes to 15 to 30 cm (6 to 12 in) from the ground after planting.

151

depending on the variety.

Pollination: Self-fertile.

Climate preferred: Cool temperate.

Aspect: Sunny or partial shade, but sheltered from strong winds.

Ideal Soil: Slightly acid, fertile soil which is well-drained.

Yield: 25 canes are sufficient for the average family.

Planting and cultivation

There are two kinds of raspberry: summer fruiting, and autumn fruiting. Both should be planted between late autumn and early spring in soil enriched with compost. Plant so that the root system is about 7.5 cm (3 in) deep and the individual canes are about 45 cm (18 in) apart. Subsequent rows of raspberries should be at least 1.2 m (4 ft) apart. Feed annually in early spring with general fertilizer at the rate of 135 gm per sq m (4 oz per sq yd). In mid-spring surround the canes with a moisture-retaining and weed-suppressing layer of compost or peat. Weeds should be kept down with either a hoe (used carefully to avoid damaging the roots) or, better still, a chemical weedkiller. Summer raspberries need support to prevent their falling over in windy weather. This is best provided by tying the canes to wires, strained horizontally between stout wooden posts at 1 m (3½ ft) and 1.5 m (5 ft) from the ground. Autumn fruiting raspberries rarely exceed 1.5 m (5 ft) and can be grown without supports.

Harvesting

Pick the fruits when they are well coloured and are easily removed from the stalks.

Pruning and training

All newly planted canes should be cut back to 15 to 30 cm (6 to 12 in) after planting. In the first summer after planting neither the summer nor

(2) Summer fruiting raspberries are pruned immediately the fruit has been harvested by cutting away all those canes which have borne fruit. Up to six of the best new canes are tied in at each plant to take their place.

(3) In late winter, summer fruiting rasp-

152

berries should be cut back slightly to around 1.65 m (5½ ft) tall to encourage the formation of fruit-bearing side-shoots.

(4) All the canes of autumn fruiting raspberries should be cut to the ground annually in late winter. Limit the number of new canes arising from each plant to six.

autumn fruiting raspberries require any pruning. All the canes of autumn fruiting raspberries should be cut to the ground annually in late winter. Summer fruiting raspberries are pruned immediately the fruit has been harvested by cutting away all those canes which have borne fruit. The new season's canes are tied in to take their place. With both autumn and summer raspberries you should limit the number of canes from any one plant to six.

Pests and diseases
Aphids, and raspberry beetle (spray with insecticide when the fruit first shows colour).

BLACKBERRY
(loganberry and boysenberry)
Size: Spread of 3.6 to 5.4 m (12 to 18 ft).
Pollination: Self-fertile.
Climate preferred: Cool temperate to subtropical.
Aspect: Any, but preferably sunny in cold, high latitude areas.
Ideal Soil: Slightly acid, fertile soil which is well-drained.
Yield: Blackberries, 9 kg (20 lb) to a plant; loganberries and boysenberries, 4 to 6 kg (9 to 13 lb) of fruit to a plant.

Planting and cultivation
It is worth making a special effort to enrich the soil for blackberries and the other hybrid berries with compost, as a single plant can yield huge quantities of fruit. The other essential is to prepare a supporting framework of supporting wires on a wall or fence. You can also strain wires horizontally at 90 cm, 1.2 m and 1.5 m (3 ft, 4 ft and 5 ft) from the ground so that you have a framework at least 4.5 m (15 ft) long. Planting can take place any time between late autumn and early spring.

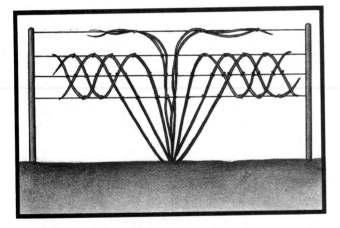

(5) Blackberries and hybrid berries should be planted in compost-enriched soil and trained against a framework of wires.

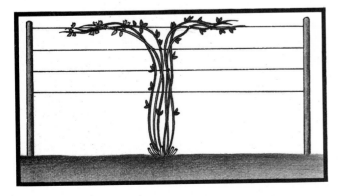

(6) Cut away the old canes at ground level

once you have harvested your crop of blackberries, loganberries or boysenberries, and tie in the new canes to take their place.

BUSH FRUITS

(1) Blackcurrants should be set in the soil so that the bushes are 5 cm (2 in) deeper than they were at the nursery. Look for the soil mark on the stem before you plant. After planting cut all the branches down to within 2.5 cm (1 in) of soil level.

153

Harvesting

Pick the fruits when they are well coloured and come away easily from the stalks.

Pruning and training

After planting, cut away the existing canes at a point 23 cm (9 in) from soil level. In future years cut away all the old canes after harvesting and tie in the new season's canes to take their place.

Pests and diseases

Aphids, and raspberry beetle (spray with insecticide when the fruit first shows colour).

BUSH FRUITS

BLUEBERRY
(highbush blueberry)

Size: 1.2 m to 1.8 m by 90 cm to 1.2 m (4 to 6 ft by 3 to 4 ft), depending on variety.
Pollination: Self-fertile.

Climate preferred: Cool temperate to temperate.
Aspect: Sunny or partial shade, but sheltered from strong winds.
Ideal Soil: Acid, peaty soil which retains moisture.
Yield: Four bushes will provide enough fruit for the average family.

Planting and cultivation

The highbush blueberry is an American relative of the European bilberry. However, its fruit is vastly superior. The soil should be prepared by adding plenty of peat, and the bushes should be planted between late autumn and early spring, spacing them 90 cm to 1.2 m (3 to 4 ft) apart. If your garden soil is alkaline, it is best to grow your blueberries in tubs 45 cm (18 in) in diameter, containing potting mixture which has been enriched with peat. In early spring give the bushes an annual feed of general fertilizer at the rate of 70 gm per sq m (2 oz per sq yd). In mid-spring surround the bushes with a thick layer of moist moss peat. If you have to water the bushes

(2) Plant red and white currants and gooseberries so that they are not quite so deep in the soil as they were at the nursery. Look for the soil mark on the stem. Unlike blackcurrants which have lots of branches arising from soil level, these bushes are grown with a distinct stem, or 'leg' as it is sometimes called.

(3) When blackcurrants are established, about a quarter of the branches should be cut down to soil level annually in autumn to encourage new fruit-producing growth.

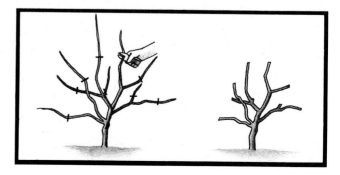

(4) The leading shoots of red and white

during dry spells, try to use water from a rainwater butt, not tap water.

Harvesting
Pick the berries while still firm for jam-making; for dessert, allow the berries to become soft and fully ripe.

Pruning and training
Pruning is unnecessary, but some of the older wood can be cut away in winter once the bushes have started to produce substantial crops.

Pests and diseases
Birds (netting is vital to protect the fruit). Otherwise trouble free.

CURRANTS
(Black, Red and White)
Size: 1.2 to 1.5 m by 90 cm (4 ft to 5 ft by 3 ft).
Pollination: Self-fertile.
Climate preferred: Cool temperate.
Aspect: Sunny or partial shade.

Ideal Soil: Any, provided it is moisture retentive and well-drained.
Yield: Four bushes will provide enough fruit for the average family.

Planting and cultivation
The soil should be well prepared by digging and working in plenty of compost or peat. Planting can be carried out between late autumn and early spring when the weather is mild and the soil is not too wet. The bushes should be spaced at least 1.2 m (4 ft) apart. Blackcurrants should be set 5 cm (2 in) deeper in the soil that they were at the nursery. Redcurrant and whitecurrants, on the other hand, are planted at the same level as at the nursery or not quite so deep in the soil. Feed each bush in early spring with general fertilizer at the rate of 135 gm per sq m (4 oz per sq yd). In mid-spring surround the bushes with a thick layer of compost or moist peat to retain moisture and to keep down weeds. The roots of currants are close to the soil surface and care must be taken when weeding not to damage them.

currants and gooseberries should be cut back **by a third to a half of their total length annually in winter. In late winter the side-shoots should be cut back to two or three buds.**

(5) Figs are best planted in pots as the restriction of the pot on the fig's roots encourages it to produce fruit. Sink the pot up to its rim in the garden soil close to a sunny wall or fence and train the branches on wires at 23 cm (9 in) intervals from the ground to a height of 1.5 m (5 ft).

(6) Bush fig trees need little pruning apart from the removal of frost-damaged and twisted shoots in mid-spring. If you wish to train a tree to a fan shape, cut the branches to the desired shape in spring. At the end of early summer, cut off the ends of the side-shoots at the fourth leaf to encourage the formation of new and further fruit-bearing side-shoots. In midsummer choose new shoots which will grow parallel to the wall, and using bamboo canes as splints, tie them into the required positions.

155

Harvesting

Pick the individual berries one at a time if you want to enjoy them at their best. Otherwise wait for two weeks after the first fruit has coloured completely before cutting away the bunches with scissors.

Pruning and training

After planting cut back all the branches of blackcurrants to within 2.5 cm (1 in) of soil level. In the first autumn after planting cut down the weakest blackcurrant shoots to soil level. In future years, once the bushes are established, cut about a quarter of the oldest branches of blackcurrants down to soil level annually in autumn to encourage renewal growth. When pruning, attempt to produce bushes with open centres which let in light and air. After planting red- and whitecurrants, all the branches should be cut back to 5 to 7.5 cm (2 to 3 in) to an outward-facing bud. In future winters cut back the leading shoots by half, and in late winter cut back the side-shoots to two or three buds.

Pests and diseases

Aphids, blackcurrant gall mites (buds in winter swell up and wither in spring—remove and burn infected growth; spray with lime sulphur when the flowers first open and repeat three weeks later), and birds (cover the bushes with netting to protect fruit buds in winter and fruit in summer).

FIG

Size: 1.2 m to 1.8 m by 90 cm to 1.2 m (4 to 6 ft by 3 to 4 ft) if grown in a pot.
Pollination: Self-fertile.
Climate: Subtropical to temperate.
Aspect: Sunny and sheltered.
Ideal Soil: Fertile and well-drained.
Yield: One bush is sufficient for most families.

Planting

Figs can be grown and ripened successfully in areas with a long and reasonably warm summer. Elsewhere you are best to grow a bush in a 25 cm (10 in) diameter pot and to stand this in a greenhouse. In fact, even outdoors you should grow your fig bush in a pot as the restriction of the pot on the fig's roots encourages it to bear fruit. Early spring is the best time for planting. The pots can either be filled with good garden soil or a proprietary potting mixture. Outdoors your fig can be planted in an ornamental pot or tub and stood on a sunny patio. If the pot has a diameter of at least 30 cm (12 in) the fig will remain bush-shaped

and grow to no more than 1.2 m (4 ft) tall. Alternatively you can plant your fig in a 45 cm (18 in) clay pot and sink this up to its rim in the garden soil close to a sunny wall or fence. The branches can then be fan-trained against wires at 23 cm (9 in) intervals from the ground to a height of 1.5 m (5 ft). A fig trained in this way should not grow to more than 1.8 m (6 ft) tall. Figs need plenty of water during late spring and summer, but feeding is not required during the first couple of years. In future years the occasional liquid feed can be given in spring and early summer.

Harvesting

Gather the figs when they are soft and the skin has just begun to split.

Pruning and training

Frost-damaged and twisted shoots should be cut away in mid-spring. If you wish to train a bush to a fan shape, cut the branches to the basic shape in early mid-spring. At the end of early summer, cut off the ends of side-shoots at the fourth leaf to encourage the formation of new and further fruit-bearing side-shoots. In midsummer select new shoots which will grow parallel to the wall and, using bamboo canes as splints, tie them into the required positions.

Pests and diseases

None of any consequence.

GOOSEBERRY

Size: 1.2 m by 90 cm (4 by 3 ft).
Pollination: Self-fertile.
Climate preferred: Cool temperate.
Aspect: Sunny or partial shade.
Ideal Soil: Any, provided that it is well-drained. Tolerant of chalky soil.
Yield: Four bushes are sufficient for the average family.

Planting and cultivation

Gooseberries can be planted any time between late autumn and early spring in soil which has been prepared by digging in plenty of compost or peat. The bushes should be set a little less deep in the soil than the nursery mark on their stems, and they should be spaced at least 1.2 m (4 ft) apart. In early spring feed them general fertilizer at the rate of 135 gm per sq m (4 oz per sq yd). In mid-spring surround the bushes with a thick layer of compost or moist peat. Take care when weeding not to damage the roots which are close to the surface.

Harvesting

Fruit for cooking should be picked while it is still firm. Fruit for eating fresh should be picked when it is soft and fully ripe.

Pruning and training

Cut back the leading shoots by half in winter; in late winter or early spring cut back the side-shoots to two or three buds. It may also be necessary to thin out the centre of the bush to let in light and air.

Pests and diseases

Aphids, American Gooseberry mildew (powdery deposit on leaves; fruit becomes brown—cut away infected shoots in autumn and spray in spring with a systemic fungicide at regular intervals), birds (bullfinches eat the fruit buds in winter—cover with netting) and sawflies.

GRAPES

GRAPES

Size: Spread of 1.2 to 6 m (4 to 20 ft), depending on the method of cultivation.
Pollination: Self-fertile.
Climate: Temperate to subtropical.
Aspect: Sunny, sheltered and ideally on a southerly slope.
Ideal Soil: Well-drained soil enriched with compost.
Yield: 0.5 kg of grapes to every 30 cm of stem (1 lb to 1 ft).

Planting and cultivation

Growing grapes is really no more difficult than growing raspberries. There are varieties for outdoors and others which are best suited to growing in a greenhouse. A vine can be trained

---

GRAPES

(1) For the first year, allow the vine against a wall to grow freely and attach the shoots loosely to a sturdy bamboo cane around 2 m (7 ft) tall. In the first autumn after planting, select the strongest two shoots and cut them back by half. All the other shoots should be cut away at the base of the vine. The two retained shoots, called 'rods', should then be attached to wires on the wall. In future autumns, after leaf-fall, these main stems or

rods should also be cut back by about half of the season's extension growth. Always cut back into ripe wood, which is a reddish brown, to a point 2.5 cm (1 in) beyond a bud. There is no point in keeping green extension growth as it will go mouldy over the winter.

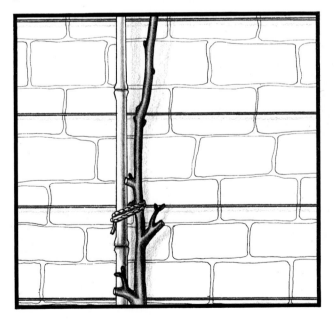

(2) The side-shoots from the main stems should also be cut back in autumn, after harvesting, to two buds. In spring when shoots form on these short spurs, the best two shoots should be retained and the others cut away.

157

on a house wall, or you can grow grapes in the open and have your own vineyard. Vines should be planted between late autumn and late winter in soil which has been well-enriched with compost. In mid-spring give the vine or vines an annual feed of general fertilizer at the rate of 135 gm per sq m (4 oz per sq yd) which should be followed by a thick layer of compost around their roots. Water thoroughly during dry spells.

Pruning and training

After planting cut the vine down to about 23 cm (9 in) from soil level. With a vine grown against a sunny wall, allow the vine during the first year to grow freely and tie the shoots to a tall bamboo cane. In autumn select the two strongest shoots and cut them back by their length. All the other shoots should be cut away at ground level. You can then put up two parallel galvanized wires 60 cm (2 ft) apart on the wall secured to 'vine eyes'. The wires

should rise vertically initially and then run horizontally. The shoots by which the vine increases in length, called 'rods', should then be lightly tied to the wires. In future years these main stems, or rods, should be allowed to grow freely, but should be cut back each autumn by about half of the season's new extension growth. See the illustrations for the full pruning routine for both outdoor and greenhouse vines.

Vines can also be grown in the open on wires stretched horizontally at 60 cm (2 ft) and 1.2 m (4 ft) from the ground. At the 1.2 m (4 ft) level the normal practice is to have wires on either side of the posts so that the upward growth of the vine can be tucked between them without the need for time-consuming tying. The vines should be planted 1.2 m (4 ft) apart and provided with a sturdy bamboo cane to support the first year's growth.

A vine can be grown quite easily in an unheated

(3) **In summer, pinch back the side-shoots growing from the spurs to two leaves beyond a bunch of fruit. Allow just one bunch of fruit to each side-shoot in the first year of fruiting. In the second year you can allow two bunches, and in the third and subsequent years of fruit three bunches can be obtained, depending on the vigour of the vine.**

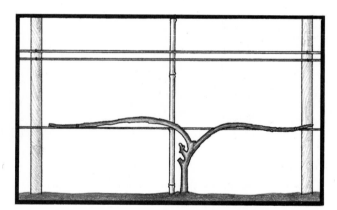

(4) **Plant vines to be grown in the open 1.2 m (4 ft) apart against a previously erected framework of wires. Each vine will need a sturdy bamboo cane to support the first season's growth. In the autumn after planting, select the two strongest shoots and cut them back to 1.2 m (4 ft). Then tie them to the lower wire on either side of the vine to make a T-shape. Cut away all the other shoots at two buds from the base of the vine. The following year, allow one bunch of grapes to each side-shoot and stop the growth at two leaves beyond this point. As with grapes on a wall, you can allow the vine to produce more grapes as it grows more vigorous. Treat the extension growths from the T-shaped rods as if they too were side-shoots.**

158

greenhouse which is at least 2.4m (8ft) long. You use basically the same method of cultivation as that for a vine on a wall outdoors, except that instead of two rods, you limit the vine to one main stem or rod. The vine must be planted outside the greenhouse, to allow its roots room to develop, and the rod led through a hole at the opposite end to the door, after a portion of the glass has been removed.

Harvesting
Leave the grapes on the vines until they are completely ripe. Then cut them from the vine with secateurs.

Pests and diseases
Birds (use netting), mildew (cut out severely infected shoots in autumn; spray throughout the season with a systemic fungicide and keep the greenhouse well ventilated) and scale insects.

RHUBARB

RHUBARB
Planting to harvest time: The plants crop in the second year onwards.
Yield: Four plants are sufficient for the average family.
Aspect: Open and sunny.
Climate preferred: Cool temperate.
Soil: Ordinary soil which has been enriched with compost.

Planting and cultivation
Rhubarb is not really fruit at all, but a vegetable stalk. Yet no one can argue about its usefulness. It is in season from early spring until the end of midsummer, and in this respect it is more than a match for most fruits. The crop is produced from rootstocks, or crowns, which are best planted in late winter or early spring. The plants are set 60 to

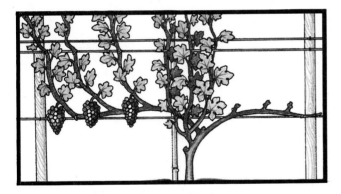

(5) The buds at the base of the vine will send up new shoots which should be secured to the cane and tucked between the topmost wires. In autumn cut away the rods which have borne fruit at two buds from the base and shorten and tie in the best two new shoots to take their place.

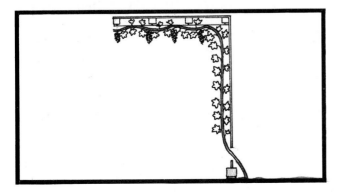

(6) If you wish to grow grapes in a greenhouse, plant the vine outside and lead one main stem through a hole in the glass at the opposite end from the door. The main stem, or rod, is allowed to extend annually vertically at first and then horizontally along a wire on the apex of the greenhouse roof. Put up also a framework of wires under the sloping roof of the greenhouse on the side which gets the sun. These wires should be spaced 30 cm (1 ft) apart.

The pruning routine for a single rod vine in a greenhouse is identical to that for a vine on a wall outdoors. Remember always to cut back the main stem back to a point 2.5 cm (1 in) beyond a bud on reddish wood. When the rod reaches the full length of the greenhouse, it too is treated as if it were a side-shoot and is trimmed back accordingly.

The side-shoots from the fruiting spurs are tied to the wires under the sloping greenhouse roof. Refer to illustrations 2 and 3 for the pruning details. In the first year of fruiting, allow only one bunch of grapes to each side-shoot: stop the growth by pinching back at the second leaf beyond each bunch of fruit. In future years you can increase your grape production according to the vigour of the vine.

159

90 cm (2 to 3 ft) apart in soil which has been well prepared by the addition of compost. The first season you should concentrate in building up the strength of the plants. So no stalks should be pulled and plenty of water should be given in dry spells. In late mid-spring surround the rhubarb with a thick layer of well-rotted compost and at the end of midsummer give the plants an annual feed of general fertilizer at the rate of 135 gm per sq m (4 oz per sq yd). Never allow flowers to form. Any which do appear should be snapped off when first seen.

Harvesting
Rhubarb should be pulled by grasping the stems low down. Do not snap stems away from the crown as the pieces left behind rot and cause damage to the rootstock. Stop pulling stems in late midsummer to allow the plants to build up their strength for the following season.

Pruning
An established rhubarb bed will give good results for up to eight years before it needs major attention. When the annual harvest is of poorer quality, the bed can be revitalized in winter by lifting the roots in winter, dividing them with a spade and replanting the best pieces.

Pests and diseases
Crown rot (shoots are thin and discoloured; rootstock develops a blackish cavity: lift and burn as there is no cure).

STRAWBERRIES

STRAWBERRY
(summer fruiting, perpetual and alpine)
Planting to harvest time: Generally three to four months. Plants have a useful life of three years.

RHUBARB

(1) **Rhubarb crowns should be planted 60 to 90 cm (2 to 3 ft) apart in late winter or early spring so that the new shoots are just showing above the soil.**

(2) **Rhubarb thrives in moist soil which is**

rich in organic matter. So in mid-spring every year surround the plants with a layer of well-rotted compost up to 15 cm (6 in) thick. This will have the effect of helping the plants to produce lots of succulent stems.

(3) **Once the annual harvest is of inferior quality, the rhubarb bed can be revitalized in winter by lifting the roots and dividing them. Simply chop each crown with a spade into several pieces. Replant the outer newer parts and discard the worn-out woody centre.**

Above: Plump, juicy strawberries.

Yield: 25 plants sufficient for average family.
Aspect: Sunny, but alpine strawberries tolerate shade.
Climate: Cool temperate to subtropical.
Ideal soil: Ordinary soil enriched with plenty of organic matter.

Planting and cultivation

There are three kinds of strawberry: the summer fruiting varieties; the perpetual fruiting varieties, which produce fruit over several months; and the alpines, which bear fruit all summer. They can be planted in spring, late summer and autumn. Late summer planting is best if you want plants which will give a superb performance the following year. Strawberries should be planted in a sunny position which has been well prepared by forking well-rotted compost or peat into the top 15 cm (6 in) of soil. No artificial fertilizers are required. Tread the soil firm and allow it to settle for a

couple of weeks before planting 45 cm (18 in) apart each way so that the crown of each plant is level with the soil surface. Water the plants well if the weather is dry. Should any plants be lifted by frost, dig them up and replant them at the correct depth. Once the flowers appear, surround the plants with a thick layer of straw or peat to keep the fruit clean. Alternatively you can surround the plants with black polythene. After fruiting, feed the plants with a proprietary tomato fertilizer which is rich in potash.

The entire stock of plants should be renewed every third year, either from your own plants or from a reputable source, and a fresh strawberry bed established in a new spot. Alpine strawberries can either be divided in early spring as you would do with an herbaceous plant, and the best pieces replanted, or you can raise new plants from seed. Alpine strawberries can also be grown as an edging to flower borders. If you want early crops of strawberries, cover the plants at the start of late winter with either cloches or polythene tunnels. Some ventilation will be necessary during the flowering period to ensure pollination.

Pruning and training
The runners from summer fruiting varieties should be cut off close to the parent plants when they appear, unless you wish to use them to increase your stock of plants. Perpetual fruiting varieties do not normally produce many runners, but those that do bear flowers and fruit and should be retained. Alpine strawberries have no runners. Summer fruiting varieties should have all their leaves cut off and the foliage burned after they finish fruiting in order to prevent disease. Perpetual fruiting strawberries should have their leaves removed in autumn. Alpines need no such treatment. If you have used straw to surround the strawberries, this should be lifted and burned.

Pests and diseases
Aphids, botrytis (grey mould), birds (protect with netting once fruit has formed), mildew, slugs, snails, strawberry caterpillars (spray with insecticide after flowering) and strawberry virus disease (leaves are small, plants are stunted: there is no cure—so dig up and burn).

STRAWBERRY

(1) If the strawberry plants are dry when you receive them, soak them in water for ten minutes. Then set the plants out so that the crown of the plant is just at ground level and the roots are well spread out. Firm the soil around the plant with your fingers. Set out other plants at a distance of 45 cm (18 in) each way.

(2) The runners from the summer fruiting

varieties should be cut off close to the parent plants when they appear, unless you wish to use them to increase your stock of plants. If you are in doubt about the health of your stock, it is far better to buy new plants from a reputable source every third year, as disease is readily transmitted from the parent plants to the runners.

(3) Summer fruiting varieties need to have all their leaves cut off and the foliage burned immediately they finish producing fruit in order to prevent disease. Remove the leaves of perpetual varieties in autumn. If you have used straw to surround the strawberries, lift this and burn it along with the leaves.

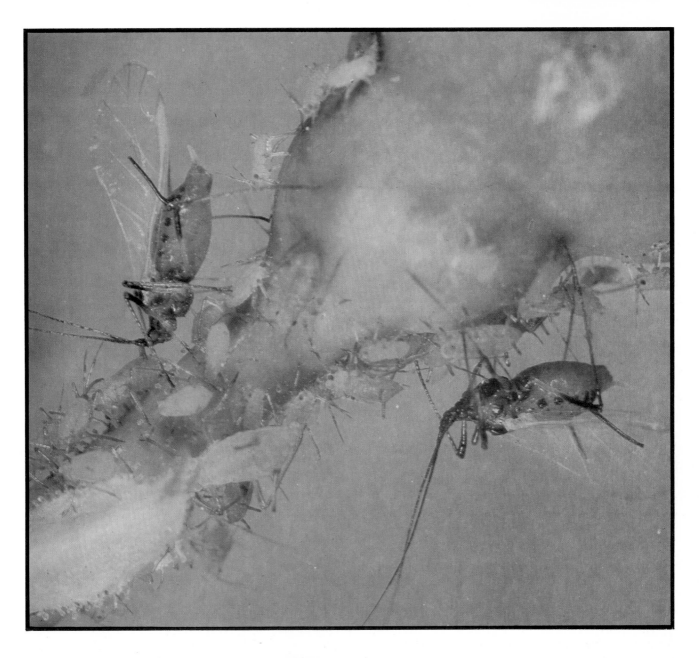

Pests
& Diseases

Once you have spent hours of hard work and given your garden a great deal of loving care, it is disheartening to find that pests and diseases have robbed you of the pleasure of seeing perfect plants, vegetables, and fruits. So it is vital to identify your enemies and to prevent them from destroying your efforts. Good garden practice, such as winter digging, rotation of vegetable crops, hoeing, feeding, and removal of garden refuse, is the best attack. Chemical control is sensible provided you always follow the manufacturers' instructions.

PROBLEMS	SYMPTOMS	TREATMENT
Aphids (greenfly, blackfly, also cream, grey, pink and brown)	Some leaves stunted and discoloured; sticky honeydew and the presence of ants; sooty mould.	Spray with a systemic insecticide on ornamental trees, shrubs and plants and fruit trees. Use a vegetable insecticide on vegetables and soft fruit.
Beetles and weevils	Holes in brassica seedling leaves, including those of radish, swede and turnip. Scalloped edges to pea and bean leaves and also those of polyanthus. Apple buds eaten with no fruit resulting.	Spray with either a vegetable or a systemic insecticide.
Birds	Leaves of lettuce and other vegetable seedlings eaten down to ground level; flower buds eaten with no fruit resulting.	Cover crop with plastic netting.
Black spot	Yellowed areas and black blotches on rose leaves which fall prematurely.	Rake up all leaves and burn. Spray with a systemic fungicide during spring and summer. If the problem is very prevalent locally, grow resistant varieties.
Botrytis (grey mould)	Leaves, stems and fruit covered with a fluffy grey mould. Fruit rots.	Spray with a systemic fungicide. Keep the moisture in frames and greenhouses drier. Outside, avoid splashing water on stems, leaves and flowers.
Cabbage root fly	Maggots eat brassica roots. The plants turn bluish, wilt and often die.	There is no cure, but the pests can be prevented by good soil cultivation and sprinkling a soil insecticide around each plant as a single dose between mid-spring and late summer.
Capsid bugs	Flattish insects, light brown or greenish in colour produce a speckled brownish pinhole appearance on leaves, shoots and fruit. The blooms of chrysanthemums and dahlias develop a lop-sided appearance.	Spray with a systemic insecticide.

PROBLEMS	SYMPTOMS	TREATMENT
Carrot fly	Maggots in roots.	There is no cure, but you can take preventive steps by delaying sowing until latish spring and burying all thinnings on the compost heap. You can also sprinkle soil insecticide along the seed drills before sowing and give a further dose in late spring, late summer, and early autumn if necessary.
Caterpillars	Holes eaten out of leaves in spring and summer.	Pick off by hand when first seen. Alternatively spray vegetables and soft fruit with vegetable insecticide; spray ornamental plants with a systemic insecticide.
Clubroot	Brassicas become stunted; the roots are distorted and swollen.	There is no cure, but the disease can be prevented by ensuring that the soil is rich in organic matter and well limed to prevent the acidic conditions which favour club root fungus. The planting holes can be dusted with calomel (mercurous chloride) when transplanting as a preventative measure.
Cutworms and leather jackets	Plants collapse with stems eaten through at, or below, ground level.	Hoe regularly to expose the pests to birds, frogs and toads. As a preventative measure soil insecticide can be sprinkled around seedlings and plants.
Damping off (fungus)	Seedlings collapse at ground level.	Use only sterile potting mixture when raising plants in clean trays and pots. Watering with the fungicide called Cheshunt compound can prevent the infection from spreading.
Earwigs	Ragged looking foliage and chewed flower petals, especially on chrysanthemums and dahlias; cobs nibbled on sweetcorn.	Drench the plants with an insecticide.

PROBLEMS	SYMPTOMS	TREATMENT
Grubs	Holes in the fruit of apples, pears and plums, peas, raspberry and blackberry.	Spray apples in early and midsummer with insecticide to kill codling moth maggots. Spray pears with a systemic insecticide when the flower buds are white to prevent maggots (pear midge). The maggots of the pea moth can be avoided by sowing in early spring; otherwise spray with insecticide in the evening when the flowers open and repeat ten days later. Maggots of the raspberry beetle can be prevented in cane fruits by spraying with a vegetable insecticide when the fruit first colours.
Leaf-cutter bees	Circular or semi-circular holes cut out of leaf margins on roses.	If the attack is severe, spray with insecticide. If not, ignore the problems as the bushes will soon grow new leaves.
Leaf hoppers	Mottled patches with a characteristic residue on the undersides of leaves of trees, shrubs and especially roses.	Spray with a systemic insecticide.
Leaf miners	Irregular channels or whitish blisters on the leaves of celery, chrysanthemums, cineraria, holly and lilac.	Spray with a systemic insecticide: celery, late spring, early and midsummer; chrysanthemums, at fourteen-day intervals all summer; holly and lilac, late spring.
Mice	Beans, peas and bulbs fail to appear, despite adequate precautions.	Bait and set traps beneath cloches. Place rodent bait inside pieces of narrow plastic piping inaccessible to domestic animals. Plant bulbs of lilies inside guards of fine wire netting.
Onion fly	Whitish maggots burrow into the base of young onion bulbs, causing wilting and the loss of plants.	There is no cure, but sow seeds in late summer or early winter to avoid the pest. Alternatively, use onion sets which are not affected.

PROBLEMS	SYMPTOMS	TREATMENT
Peach leaf curl	Leaf curl with crimson blistering at first followed by a thickening of the foliage which turns white before falling. Almond, peach and nectarine are all susceptible.	Spray with lime sulphur when the leaves are dropping in autumn and repeat again at bud burst in late winter or early spring.
Powdery mildew	Upper and lower leaf surfaces are covered with a white deposit which may cause distortion.	Roses should be sprayed regularly with a systemic fungicide to keep them clear of infection. Spray other plants when the disease is first noticed. The infection can be largely avoided by keeping the soil moist and by applying a mulch around roots in mid-spring.
Red Spider mite	Microscopic mites cause pale mottling on the leaves of greenhouse trees and plants and outdoors in summer on roses, strawberries and other plants.	Keep a more humid atmosphere in greenhouses; otherwise spray with malathion or systemic insecticide.
Root aphid	Whitish mealy pests on roots of lettuce cause the plants to wilt.	Surround plants with a light sprinkling of soil insecticide.
Rust	Black or rust coloured spores on the undersides of antirrhinum, carnation, hollyhock, mint, plum and roses. Leaves fall prematurely.	Spray roses with rose fungicide regularly. Spray other plants with liquid copper fungicide and repeat weekly if necessary.
Scale insects	Tiny shell-like insects on fruit trees, ornamental trees, shrubs and greenhouse pot plants. Sooty moulds on stems.	Spray with systemic insecticide three times at fourteen-day intervals.
Slugs and snails	Leaves chewed; faint silvery trails around plants.	Keep the garden tidy and free from decaying matter. Surround susceptible seedlings and plants with slug bait.
Thrips (thunderflies)	Silver mottling and severe distortion of shoots on greenhouse plants, gladioli, onions and peas.	Spray with a systemic or vegetable insecticide.

INDEX

Page numbers in **bold** refer to photographs. Numbers in *italics* refer to step-by-step illustrations.